Rebellion, Remorse, and Return

The Prodigal Son's Painful Journey Home

John A. Stroman

CSS Publishing Company, Inc., Lima, Ohio

Copyright © 2004 by
CSS Publishing Company, Inc.
Lima, Ohio

Scripture quotations are from the *New Revised Standard Version of the Bible*, copyright 1989 by the Division of Christian Education of the National Council of the Churches of Christ in the USA. Used by permission.

Library of Congress Cataloging-in-Publication Data

Stroman, John A.
    Rebellion, remorse, and return : the prodigal son's painful journey home / John A. Stroman.
        p. cm.
Includes bibliographical references (p.   ).
    ISBN 0-7880-1996-1 (pbk.)
    1. Bible. N.T. Luke XV, 11-32—Criticism, interpretation, etc. 2. Bible. N.T. Luke XV, 11-32—Criticism, interpretation, etc. 3. Prodigal son (Parable) I. Title.
BS2595.53.S77 2004
226.8'06—dc22

                                                                        2003021718

For more information about CSS Publishing Company resources, visit our website at www.csspub.com or e-mail us at custserv@csspub.com or call (800) 241-4056.

ISBN 0-7880-1996-1

To my grandchildren,
J.D., Meghan, Christine, and Zhen Zhen

Regardless ... there will always be a homecoming!

Other Books By John A. Stroman

Tongues Of Fire

God's Downward Mobility

Out Of The Whirlwind

Ashes To Ascension

Thunder From The Mountain:
The Ten Commandments For Today

Pray In This Way: Sermons On The Lord's Prayer

I am the prodigal son every time I search for unconditional love where it cannot be found. Why do I keep ignoring the place of true love and persist in looking for it elsewhere?

— Henri J. M. Nouwen

The Parable Of The Prodigal Son

Then Jesus said, *"There was a man who had two sons. The younger of them said to his father, 'Father, give me the share of the property that belongs to me.' So he divided his property between them. A few days later the younger son gathered all he had and traveled to a distant country, and there he squandered his property in dissolute living. When he had spent everything, a severe famine took place throughout that country, and he began to be in need. So he went and hired himself out to one of the citizens of that country, who sent him to his fields to feed the pigs. He would gladly have filled himself with the pods that the pigs were eating; and no one gave him anything. But when he came to himself, he said, 'How many of my father's hired hands have bread enough and to spare, but here I am dying of hunger! I will get up and go to my father, and I will say to him, "Father, I have sinned against heaven and before you; I am no longer worthy to be called your son; treat me like one of your hired hands."' So he set off and went to his father. But while he was still far off, his father saw him and was filled with compassion; he ran and put his arms around him and kissed him. Then the son said to him, 'Father, I have sinned against heaven and before you; I am no longer worthy to be called your son.' But the father said to his slaves, 'Quickly, bring out a robe — the best one — and put it on him; put a ring on his finger and sandals on his feet. And get the fatted calf and kill it, and let us eat and celebrate, for this son of mine was dead and is alive again; he was lost and is found!' And they began to celebrate.*

"Now the elder son was in the field; and when he came and approached the house, he heard music and dancing. He called one of the slaves and asked what was going on. He replied, 'Your brother has come, and your father has killed the fatted calf, because he got him back safe and sound.' Then he became angry and refused to go in. His father came out and began to plead with him. But he answered his father, 'Listen! For all these years I have been working like a slave for you, and I have never disobeyed your command; yet you have never given me even a young goat so that I might celebrate with my friends. But when this son of yours came back, who has devoured your property with prostitutes, you killed the fatted calf for him!' Then the father said to him, 'Son, you are always with me, and all that is mine is yours. But we had to celebrate and rejoice, because this brother of yours was dead and has come to life; he was lost and has been found.'"

— Luke 15:11-32

Table Of Contents

Preface

Joseph Campbell said, "It is by going down into the abyss that we discover the treasures of life." Here is the story of a young man going down into the abyss. The story of the prodigal is a contemporary story. It is the life passage of so many: rebellion, rejection, running away, the pain of homesickness, and finally discovery and homecoming. However, not everyone finds their way back. Many die in a distant land without hope. The prodigal, in losing all he had, discovered the value of what he had. The tragedy is, for all his pain, suffering, and humiliation, what he was searching for he already had before he left, but it took the experience in a distant land for him to make that discovery. He was convinced that happiness was somewhere else.

The prodigal follows the same road that sons and daughters have traveled for centuries. It has been repeated ever since there have been parents and children. It is foremost a parable about God who is revealed in the actions of a compassionate parent. Jesus, by dramatizing a family tragedy, focuses on the crisis of broken relationships between human beings and God. A person living without God is like a younger son running away to a far country. The message is clear: there is no land so distant, no sin so degrading, no rebellion so strong or defiant to erase the fact that God still loves all of his children and we can come home. Regardless!

The story does not end with the younger son's return, but rather with the refusal of the elder son to come in and enjoy the party celebrating his brother's return. This is an important part of the story because it is the part that deals with most of us. Most of us did not travel to a distant land. We just stayed home and pouted. Not all prodigals leave home; some remain and become strangers in their own home.

During the period of preparing this manuscript two traumatic events shook our nation and world and have forever reshaped our lives. First, the events of September 11, 2001, occurred. One moment the World Trade Center was there and then it and nearly 4,000 lives were gone. One moment we were a nation of peace and prosperity and then we became a nation of war and recession. At one moment secure, fixed, and reliable, the world suddenly appeared more fragile than ever. Like the prodigal, we lost our way — staggering and stunned. The cry we heard over and over was, "Oh, my God! Oh, my God!" Many asked, "Where is God?" When we collected our thoughts, we realized that God was where God has always been, loving and caring for all creation.

Second, the war with Iraq in 2003 has caused many in the Christian community to rethink their position on war and violence. The parable reminds us that God's love and grace are the most stable factors in all of God's world. In the midst of the indescribable pain and suffering these two devastating events have caused, the theme of the parable is caught up in the words of George Matheson's hymn, "O love that wilt not let me go, I rest my weary soul in thee." This ancient story in Luke 15 is being played out in our world, and we need to tell it again with the hope that some may find their way home to a God of infinite love and grace.

Much of this book's research was done when I taught a class on the Parables of Jesus at Trinity Theological Seminary, Ghana, West Africa. Over the last couple of years, much fresh work has gone into the manuscript. I hope this material will be beneficial to pastors, teachers, and laity who take biblical studies seriously.

Each chapter is divided into two parts, Commentary and Reflections, and each ends with Discussion Questions. The Commentary section is an exegetical approach to the text. The Reflections section deals with the textual issues within the Commentary geared especially to contemporary concerns. This section provides numerous possibilities for teaching and preaching in light of the text. It is intended to stimulate the thought and the imagination of both the teacher and the preacher.

The Introduction contains a rather definitive statement regarding Jesus' use of parables. In the Appendix is additional information regarding The Task of Interpretation. At the end is a detailed bibliography for those who desire to do further study.

John A. Stroman
Tallahassee, Florida

Introduction

Jesus' Use Of Parables

Before we begin our study of the Parable of the Prodigal Son let us take time to consider Jesus' use of parables. The parables of Jesus in the New Testament create for us immediate and vivid images in our minds. They possess an arresting quality that is etched deeply into our memory. It is remarkable how we can recall most of them with an astonishing accuracy. The reason the common people were so receptive of Jesus' words, "and the large crowd was listening to him with delight" (Mark 12:37), was because they identified with the images that his parables created. The parables were based on images and stories that were visible and well-known to the listener. Because Jesus' parables dealt with familiar ideas, they ignited an instinctive recognition in the hearts and minds of the masses.

Let the word *parable* be spoken and certain distinct pictures come to mind. It brings immediately to mind a man who fell among thieves, a rejoicing shepherd who is returning from an all-night search with the lost sheep across his shoulders, or the graphic picture of an elderly father looking down a distant path for the return of a wayward son. Hardly a week goes by without hearing or reading a quote from one of Jesus' parables. How often have you heard such phrases as "acting like a good Samaritan," "passing by on the other side," or those who indulge "in riotous living"? There are those who used their "talents wisely" while others "hide them under a bushel." Before we launch a new program or plan a trip, we are admonished to "count the cost" and never leave things until the "eleventh hour." These phrases and many more from Jesus' parables are part of our everyday speech. The parables to some degree are ever present with us. Stories by their very nature are easier to remember than mere facts or abstract statements. They provide us with unforgettable pictures and images that can be recalled long after the words of more abstract teachings have been forgotten. Scholars have long agreed that the parables are the closest one can get to Jesus' original teachings.

The remarkable thing about Jesus' use of parables is the number of occasions in which he was recalling, especially to the Jewish community, that which they already knew. It was not strange or unfamiliar information to them. For the Jewish mind, the world stood steadfast on three basic principles: justice, truth, and peace. Jesus knew this and through his use of parables he brought this to their minds. I am certain that Jesus was aware of how Nathan, the prophet, was determined to confront David with the message of God's judgment for his murder of Uriah and the theft of his wife. Jesus knew how Nathan made such powerful use of a parable regarding the rich man's flock and the poor man's lamb in order to bring justice and judgment to David.

What Is A Parable?

Parable means a comparison, an analogy, or to "set along side." It is a comparison drawn from nature or daily life and designed to illumine some spiritual truth, on the assumption that what is valid in one sphere is valid in another. Therefore, parable is a teaching form. Almost all teaching consists in comparing the unknown with the known, the strange with the familiar. How many times in our discussions with one another do we seek to gain understanding by making comparisons? This is almost a daily experience for most of us. How often Jesus would begin a parable by saying, "The kingdom of God is like...."

Basically, a parable is a story that is or may be true and is used generally to teach some moral or religious truth. Its purpose is to teach one point and the details of the story are subordinate to that one point. The essential meaning of a parable can become obscure if too much emphasis is placed on the details. Such attention to the details can end up in an intricate unreality, causing the essential meaning of the parable to be lost. Recent biblical scholarship suggest that a parable does not have one point, but it is the point.

In contrast to a parable, *allegory* personifies more abstract things. In an allegory there is not one central meaning, but every detail of the story has some parallel meaning. Allegory is a kind of "descriptive code" and if it is to be fully understood, it must be deciphered point by point, feature by feature. Whereas, in the parable there is one chief point of likeness between the story and the meaning and the details simply help make the story realistic and so serve the central thrust of the parable. In the allegory things are not what they appear to be, but in the parable things are what they profess to be. Throughout the church's history there has been the temptation to treat parable as allegory, especially by those who were convinced that Jesus' parables were coded because of his words in Mark 4:10-12. The classic illustrations of allegorical interpretation are the two great Church Fathers: Augustine and Tertillian. Augustine turned the parable of the Good Samaritan into an amazing allegorical interpretation. Tertillian did the same in his sermon on the parable of the Prodigal Son.

Other literary forms that resemble parable are *simile* and *metaphor*. A simile is a statement of likeness in literal terms. So when Jesus said, "The kingdom of heaven is like yeast that a woman took and mixed with three measures of flour until all was leavened" (Matthew 13:3), appears to be simile and no more. A *metaphor* is a figure of speech that taxes the imagination by saying that the first object is the second, or speaking as though it were. Such use of metaphors by Jesus are found in the Gospel of John, where Jesus said, "I am the door" (John 10:7). "I am the living bread" (John 6:51). "I am the good shepherd" (John 10:11). "I am the way" (John 14:6). Although other forms of communication were available to Jesus, the parable is undoubtedly the best technique that he used.

Although Jesus did not create the parable, in a sense he perfected it as a method of teaching. The parables contain Jesus' most memorable messages, and they are still etched in our recollection long after a sermon has become blurred and forgotten. Virtually nothing that Jesus said is recorded in lecture form. Nearly all of his teaching and preaching was in parable-story form. For Jesus this form of teaching had power, "for he taught them as one having authority ..." (Matthew 7:29). In the parables of the New Testament we are dealing with a particularly trustworthy tradition and we are brought immediately into a relationship with Jesus. These parables are important for the Christian church because they represent Jesus' basic message and present us with the permanent challenge and hope of the Christian understanding of existence. We experience in Jesus' parables what William Willimon calls the *reversal of expectation*, causing the dislocation of the hearer. Just when the hearer has lowered his guard feeling that he has things pretty well figured out, then zap — with a sword-like thrust the parable drives its message home, leaving the hearer defenseless. When first hearing a parable, it sounds like one of those peasant yarns, but it keeps something up its sleeve, and then it pops with such a force that it leaves the hearer speechless and flat. Although there are those parables that come with the force of a solemn warning and heart-searching accusations, let us not overlook those parables of Jesus that reveal the gentle and gracious assurance of God's love and grace. Robert Farrar Capon has helped us make this distinction with his two volumes on the parables titled *The Parables of Judgment* and *The Parables of Grace.*

There Were Parables Before Jesus

Parables can be found in the Old Testament and in the extra-canonical writings of the Jews and in the literature of other ancient peoples. Possibly, Jesus first heard men reciting parables in the synagogue and he was well aware of the parables of the Old Testament. He knew the powerful effect they had upon their hearers. The genius of Jesus was his ability to use an old pattern and bring to mind new ideas and teachings that caused his hearers to have an immediate identification. A favorite formula of rabbinical teaching has been, "What shall I liken it?" Jesus used the parable to *"liken it"* in the language of the masses. Jesus' uniqueness was his ability to adapt a well-known parable or story and retell it in a vivid, memorable, and powerful way. He took an old form and gave it new life.

It has been pointed out that the difference between rabbinical parables and those of Jesus is precisely the difference between their mind and his mind. Even at their best, the rabbinical stories lack the inevitability of the parables of Jesus. The difference was one of authority. Jesus' authority seems to rest on his incorporation of truth and love. For Jesus there is a close relationship between faith and ethics, belief and practice, between what he spoke and how he lived.

Not only did Jesus know the parables of the Old Testament, but he knew the Jewish mind and how reality is approached. For the Hebrew mind truth could be seen in some fact of the familiar world. Truth is so substantial that it feeds the imagination and does not merely outline an idea. For instance, Old Testament writers did not create creedal statements. When they came to declare the providence of God, they simply said, "The Lord is my shepherd" (Psalm 23:1). They did not speculate on human religious impulse, but said, "As a deer longs for flowing streams, so my soul longs for you, O God" (Psalm 42:1). They did not give a treatise on the importance of heredity, but merely stated, "The parents have eaten sour grapes, and the children's teeth are set on edge" (Ezekiel 18:2). The same theme is seen in the discourse following the second commandment, "punishing children for the iniquity of parents, to the third and fourth generations of those who reject me, but showing steadfast love to the thousandth generation of those who love me and keep my commandments" (Exodus 20:5-6). Jesus understood the prophet's and psalmist's way of thinking. He felt his truth intuitively and set it out in vivid symbols and stories that all people would understand. Jesus seemed to sense that his hearers did not comprehend mere cold hard facts about truth, but were able to grasp truth that was presented in mental pictures and stories. The masses wanted to see the truth, so Jesus presented it to them in a form that they could see and not forget.

Jesus did not create his parables from scratch. He chose stories from common human experiences: the relationship of family members, the way people behave in the business world, the life of farmers and shepherds, and the way people worshiped and lived out their religious life. Unfortunately for us, all of Jesus' parables are on the printed page. It is a pity that they did not have video cameras in the first century, so we could actually see Jesus before the crowd, listen to his voice, see the expression on his face, and follow the movement of his hands. All of that is lost to us and we need to visualize these realities in order to capture the full meaning of the parables. Only by the use of our imagination can we hear what they heard. That is the uniqueness of the parables that come to us on the written page — their ability to stimulate the imagination.

What About Mark 4:10-14?

What did Jesus mean by this passage?

> *When he was alone, those who were around him along with the twelve asked him about the parables. And he said to them, "To you has been given the secret of the kingdom of God but for those outside, everything comes in parables, in order that they may indeed look, but not perceive and may indeed listen, but not understand: so that they may not turn again and be forgiven."*

This is one of those most difficult passages in the New Testament to interpret. At face value this passage seems to suggest that Jesus used parables to conceal rather than reveal truth. One scholar has suggested that the use of the word for *parable* in the Old Testament means exactly that. The Hebrew word for parable is *mashal,* which not only means "to be like," but can also have the meaning of an oracle, riddle, or a saying so dark and mysterious that it will not be understood. "I will open my mouth in parable, I will utter dark sayings from old" (Psalm 78:2). With this Old Testament understanding is it possible that Jesus intended his parables to give meaning that only his disciples and closest followers could understand, while the crowd was left in bewilderment? Those in the early church felt this was so, causing them to follow an allegorical interpretation giving the parables a secret and coded message.

In the text is a quotation from Isaiah 6:9-10. Some have suggested that these verses contain the conclusions that the prophets arrived at later after long years of bitter opposition. After all of Isaiah's efforts the people had rejected the word of the Lord. The prophet seems to regard this rejection on the part of the people as the will of God. Much of the same thought seems to be in Mark's mind. When Mark saw how Jesus had been rejected and finally crucified, looking back on this event, it could be that he felt from the beginning that the masses never understood or appreciated the teachings of Jesus and from the beginning God never expected them to understand. In retrospect, this may have been what Mark thought, but not necessarily what Jesus thought. It appears to me that the overall message of the scriptures emphasizes that Jesus came to enlighten and not darken the human mind. He spoke in parables for the very purpose of knowing that they would bring hope and meaning to all who heard them. There is no evidence in the reading of scripture that Jesus sought to hide or obscure the truth in the use of parables.

William Barclay makes an interesting comment regarding this passage. He suggests that it should be read not in a bitter tone, but with the tone of regretful love, then it will sound quite differently. Jesus used parables to communicate truth, but at the same time he saw in the eyes of many of his listeners the lack of understanding. He was aware that many never comprehended what he was saying to them. He felt their rejection and lack of comprehension. Therefore, his words were not spoken as a result of anger, but disappointment. Here was one who had so much to give, but the people were too blind, too busy, too preoccupied to give it any thought or consideration. Jesus spoke out of a frustrated love. I think it is absurd to think that Jesus deliberately used the parables to conceal the truth from those who were not his disciples. The ultimate purpose of Jesus' use of parables is to reveal, to illumine, and to save.

What The Parables Reveal About Jesus

When we study the parables we are looking into the most revealing apertures of Jesus' teaching and person. In the parables, it is not so much that we are instructed by Jesus but that we stand with him and view life through his eyes. The parables give us clues about what Jesus is interested in and areas in which his mind is moving. Many themes in his parables and teachings center around his early years of growing up in his family. He came as an infant laid in his mother's arms. He grew up as a little boy, looked up into his mother's eyes, and reached out for her hand and followed

19

her footsteps. Many of Jesus' parables came from this mother-son relationship. As a tiny child he remembered how his mother's fingers would knead the yeast into the dough and with a child's fascination watched how it was transformed before his eyes. He saw on numerous occasions his mother mend their precious clothing, until the time came when a new patch could no longer be placed on an old piece of clothing.

Often he accompanied his mother to the public well in Nazareth, and it was there that he understood the meaning of being grateful for a cup of cold water taken from his mother's hand. It could be that he was thinking about his mother the time he told the parable about the woman who lost the coin. He would have remembered how every penny was precious in his home, especially after his father's death, because his mother had the responsibility of raising the family. Possibly, he remembered when his mother lost a coin and how frantically the entire family searched for it and what celebration they had when they found it. It could be that he was remembering his father Joseph and what an influence he had on him in those early years, when he said to a crowd of parents, "If you then, who are evil, know how to give good gifts to your children ..." (Matthew 7:11).

Jesus' early life in Nazareth absorbed all the sights and sounds of life, from the hills and fields that surrounded it, to those simple and homely things that meant nothing then, but were to mean so much more later. Those early years were woven deeply into his memory — the Galilean meadows with their wild lilies, a hen gathering her young chicks, a wild bird building its nest in a bush, the springtime sowing of the seed, and the fall harvest of separating the wheat from the chaff, children playing in the marketplace, the formation of storm clouds in the summertime, and a shepherd going off to look for a lost lamb. Jesus knew what was in the hearts and minds of women and men, because he knew life as they knew life — in all of its beauty and stark reality.

In Jesus' parables we see people that Jesus saw and we see what these people meant to him. Jesus craved human companionship. It is remarkable that not only did Jesus know fisherman, but that they were his friends and he felt no strangeness or awkward-ness about them. He shared dinner with Matthew and Zacchaeus who were tax collectors and there was no feeling of constraint on his part. He took his food gladly with the rich and the poor. He did something that the church finds difficult to do today: he minis-tered to both extremes of society, the rich and the poor. All life drew him with great instinctive sympathy and feeling. The parables bear witness to the intensity of the interest, love, and compassion that Jesus possessed when he looked upon this world.

Chapter One

Why Is Happiness Always Somewhere Else?

Then Jesus said, "There was a man who had two sons. The younger of them said to his father, 'Father, give me the share of the property that will belong to me.' So he divided his property between them."   — Luke 15:11-12

Commentary

Scholars point out that the request by the younger son seemed inappropriate for a first-century Jewish son, who like most sons at that time, knew the provisions of the mishnaic law (Brad Young, *The Parables of Jesus*, p. 138). The custom regarding inheritance was well known by Jewish families because inheritance was a critical question constantly being dealt within the Jewish community. Therefore, the son could not declare innocence as a result of ignorance.

It was not unusual for a Jewish father to draw up a testament regarding his property. What is unusual was for the father to allot to his younger son his portion prior to his death. A son by request could acquire title to his father's property, but the interest on the property would continue to come to the father until his death. Or, if the son sold the property, the purchaser would only take possession of it upon the death of the father.

Much has been written by scholars regarding the son's request and the father's action. Craig Blomberg has pointed out that the parable is not as lifelike as many have alleged (*Interpreting the Parables*, p. 176). He asks, would a first-century Jewish son have dared to ask his father for his share of the inheritance while the father is still in good health? Would the father have capitulated so readily? Probably not. Most agree that such behavior was deplorable. Kenneth Bailey goes so far as to interpret the son's request as equivalent to a death wish. He suggests that he was looking forward to his father's death with eager anticipation. If that is so, then the father's response is an incredible expression of grace and love (*Poet and Peasant*, p. 161). Other commentators have pointed out that the father's action was inappropriate. "The father who gives into his son is a fool" (Blomberg, p. 176). The thought is that by the son's action the father's place was usurped by his son and the father's authority and honor have been compromised.

Ibrahim Sa'id, from his cultural study of this parable, suggests that "the shepherd in search of the sheep, the woman in search of the coin, do not do anything out of the ordinary beyond what anyone in their place would do. But the actions the father takes in the third story (in Luke 15) are unique, marvelous, divine actions which have not been done by any father in the past" (*Commentary on Luke*, p. 395). I stated in the introduction that the father reveals God's love as seen through Christ and this is the lens through which we must view this parable. Therefore, this is not your ordinary father.

Verse 12 states, "So he divided his property between them." Between whom? It was between the elder son and the younger son. It is in this verse that the nature of the elder son emerges. On hearing that he gets his share of the inheritance as well, which is two-thirds of the inheritance since he is the elder son, he remains silent. The hearers would have expected a loud cry of protest from the elder son. This is the customary role for the elder son to play — protecting and defending his father. To the amazement of all, he remains silent. There is no doubt that the elder son's silence shouts out loud at the first-century audience. They were saying to themselves, "In the name of decency, say something." But he never spoke a word. Scholars have pointed out that he is shameless and disloyal. Bailey states that even the father is suspect, since he gives in without any protest (p. 68). Even the villagers probably wondered about the sanity and functionality of this family. In order to understand the relationship between the family and the village, one needs to know something about the first-century Palestine ceremony of *qesasah*. Bailey describes the background and significance of this ceremony:

*From the Jerusalem Talmud it is known that the Jew of
the time of Jesus had a method for punishing any Jewish boy who lost the family inheritance to Gentiles. It
was called the* qesasah *ceremony. Horror at such a
loss is also reflected in the Dead Sea Scrolls. Such a
violator of community expectations would face the*
qesasah *ceremony if he dared to return to his home
village. The ceremony is simple. The villagers would
bring a large earthenware jar, fill it with burned nuts
and burned corn, and break it in front of the guilty
individual. While doing this, the community would
shout, "So and so is cut off from his people." From
that point on, the village would have nothing to do with
the wayward lad.* — Poet and Peasant, *p.* 167f

When the villagers discover what is taking place in the family
they may well "break the jar in the streets" and cut off the younger
son from the community.

It was evident to all that there were serious rifts and disagree-
ments both within the family and the village. The tension that is
developing within the story is what makes the story so magnificent and compelling. In regard to the harshness of the younger
son's action, Bernard Scott points out that first-century Palestine
was a place of little opportunity. Life was brutal and harsh. It was
natural that younger sons would cash in on their inheritance and
go take their chances in a foreign land (*Hear Then the Parables*, p.
109).

In these first two brief verses we are introduced to the entire
cast of three people and all three play a very important role in the
drama. The audience expected the actors to play a different role.
Brad Young points out that "Jesus loves to use reversal roles in his
parabolic teachings to break normal reactions" (*The Parables of
Jesus*, p. 140). Jesus skillfully uses this method to surprise his listeners and get their attention. Scholars call this tactic of Jesus the
reversal of expectation, causing the dislocation of the hearer. Just
when the hearer has lowered his guard feeling that he has things
pretty well figured out, then zap — with a sword-like thrust the
parable drives its message home, leaving the hearer defenseless.

An interesting twist is given to this part of the parable by William Willimon, Dean of the Chapel at Duke University. He suggests that this parable is an image of our maturation which is most congenial to our society and that America was built by immigrants, people who left their parents to seek their fortune in a distant land of the New World. They in turn taught their children that the only way to get ahead was to immigrate, to leave home, severing parental ties. Willimon suggests, being a campus minister, that the *far country* is the average college campus where everyone is forced to abandon their parents and the church in order to grow up. He suggests that in today's world, the path to maturation comes not only from the college experience, but also from the influence of corporations who require their people to be ready to move at the drop of a hat. They need people who will move at a moment's notice, who are trained to subordinate family, traditions, friends, and values to the demands of the corporation. Willimon concludes that "such people are better managed than those who must still answer to the old man" (*Pulpit Resources*, January '95, p. 52).

Other writers have similar views as Willimon. One is the French writer Andre Gide who invents another ending to the parable, having the returning son sending his older brother into the far country so that he too can grow up and mature. Gide suggests that it is good for a son to be lost for a while. He feels it is good for him to rebel and sin, because everyone has to go through this sometime in life. He concludes that in the life of every son and daughter there is rebellion; this is one of life's essential passages.

The listeners, as they were drawn into the narrative, felt that they had pretty much figured things out. They probably expected the younger son to die of hunger. When he left home, they knew he would never come back. The father would never see him again. In their eyes, this was a punishment well-deserved. They probably expected the elder son to act as a mediator and defend his father's honor, because this was the normal role expected of the elder son. To their utter surprise he becomes disloyal and shameful in his actions regarding his father. What were their expectations of the father? No doubt they expected him to bring severe punishment against his abusive son who brought him such dishonor and public disgrace. This was completely justifiable punishment as far as the hearers were concerned because the two sons had broken the fifth commandment — a commandment held with the highest esteem within the Jewish community. The audience is completely caught off guard by the father's compassion. Young concludes, "the plot of the story and the unexpected reversal of roles makes for a lively drama that captures the attention of the listeners and leads them to embrace the type of love that comes from God alone" (Young, p. 140). For those listening to this drama unfold, the greatest surprise of all is that Jesus is laying down the fundamental principle that God loves the sinner — whether he travels to a distant land and loses it all or remains at home and becomes a stranger within his own house.

Reflections

Things were getting on the younger son's nerves. The discipline of his father was becoming unbearable and, he felt, unreasonable. This coupled with the tediousness of his dull older brother was more than he could stand. He needed his space. He craved freedom from it all. At every turn he found himself tripping over barriers and signboards of restraint. He felt he had had enough and now was the time to make the break.

In my mind's eye I can imagine the dialogue that may have gone something like this, the son saying to his father, "I want my freedom. I can't go on like this anymore. These everlasting restraints and restrictions, telling me constantly what I can and cannot do are more than I can bear. I need my space."

The father is silent. His son anxiously awaits his response. But his father keeps busy as though he did not hear him. The son is annoyed by his father's apparent disregard. Finally, his father looks up and breaks the silence by saying, "So, you think you have no freedom. You are my son. You can come and go as you please. You can tell me everything or anything that is troubling you. Look, what I have I share with you. I always have. You are free — subject to no one. You give account only to me. Isn't that freedom?"

"No!" his son responds. "To be honest with you, I don't give a hoot for all of this! Freedom is to do what I want to do, when I want to do it. Accountable to no one!"

The father responds in a deliberate, matter-of-fact manner by saying, "We have differences of opinion regarding freedom. For me, freedom means that you should be free to be what you ought to be and are — a son. My son. Freedom is to allow me to be your father. In your desire to be free, don't become a slave — a slave to your desires, ambitions, and the need for recognition."

The son leaves his father, goes off to the barn, and climbs up in the hayloft to be alone. He says to himself, "He wants me to ignore my ambitions, desires, my need for recognition. These are the very things that are important to me. The old man doesn't understand. These are the very things I cannot ignore. I have a tremendous desire to live. I crave recognition for what I do and for who I am. Is that so bad? I'll show him that I can do it on my own. All I want is this one time, this one opportunity to prove myself and then I'll come back. Now I need a break, to get away to a place where God, church, and family don't matter." Within he could feel his pulses beating, his passions seething, along with an elemental force of a healthy vitality straining for expression. He is convinced that there is nothing wrong in letting all of this out and express how he really feels.

A short time later the father and his sons finished their chores and were quietly eating their dinner together. The younger son looks up from his eating and interrupts the silence by saying to his father, "Tomorrow, Father, I am leaving home." The elder son, in disbelief, drops his hands to the table and stares at his father, waiting for his reply.

For several moments the father sits motionless looking at his son without moving or saying a word. Then in a soft, calm low tone he asks him, "What did you say?"

"I said that I am leaving home," the son replied. "I know that this is a strange request, but would you consider giving me the portion of the family estate that belongs to me? I don't think this is unreasonable since it really does belong to me."

The son is treating his father with disrespect through his request. He is breaking deep and sacred Hebrew family ties and is treating his father as though he were already dead. In essence, the son is saying to his father, "Drop dead! Father, I cannot wait for you to die." The request is cruel and reveals a profound break between the son and his father. The lack of sensitivity at this point, on the son's part, suggests he is lost indeed. He is lost to feeling, respect, and reality. The reality is that he is oblivious to his father's love and care for all these years, as well as, his failure to understand his father's need for financial support in his old age.

It is said we often hurt those who love us the most and often are unconscious of how deeply we have hurt them. How true this was for the prodigal. It appears by all evidence that the son's actions echoed a death wish toward his father. His cold-hearted request was an act of painful rejection and rebellion. At this early stage of rebellion, he is not aware of the magnitude of his defiant action. It took the painful journey into a distant land to bring this to his consciousness.

William Barclay tells the story that in Hitler's Germany a man was arrested because he stood for freedom. He endured imprisonment and torture with great courage. Finally, with his spirit still unbroken he was released. A short time afterwards he committed suicide. Many wonder why. Those who knew him well knew the reason. They had discovered that his son was the one who had informed against his father. Barclay said treachery of his own son broke him in a way that the cruelty of his enemies was unable to achieve (Barclay, *The Gospel of Mark*, p. 313).

The prodigal's actions and words brought anguish to his father that was extremely difficult. It is one thing for a person to wish for your death, but when it is your son's desire, it causes pain that is impossible to bear. Two things stand out: the father's silence and the fact that he grants the son's request. In the Middle Eastern milieu, the father is expected to explode and discipline the boy for the cruel implications of his demand. Here is a dramatic illustration of the quality of love that grants freedom at the expense of rejecting the lover.

Without saying a word, the father gets up from his chair and leaves the room. The two brothers continue to eat together in silence. The elder son is still in shock and can't believe what he has just heard. Soon the father enters the room and gives to each of his sons a small leather bag containing their portions of the family inheritance — "so he divided his property between them" (v. 12). The elder son is given two-thirds and the younger son one-third. There is no argument. No pleas are made for his younger son to stay. He merely gives his sons their share of the property and to the younger son his freedom to leave.

Many have suggested that it was foolhardy for the father to grant his son's request. To jeopardize his financial support in his old age is something no father would do, especially amid the hard conditions of first-century Palestine. The listeners must be shaking their heads in disbelief saying, "What a foolish man." For the listeners, severe punishment or complete rejection would not be out of the question. To the surprise of all, the father grants the son's request. The more the parable unfolds, the clearer the father's love becomes. One central point that Jesus wants to get across in this parable is that this is not your ordinary father. The action of the father, being both amazing and surprising, certainly caught the attention of the listeners.

It is difficult for us to understand the cultural setting in which this story is taking place, especially its impact on the village. The role between the family and the community is a very important one. When the villagers discover what is taking place in the family, they may well cut the younger son off from the community. This may be difficult for us to comprehend, but what the son has done to his father is of serious consequence to the village. The son is not only breaking off relationship with his family, but in a radical way with the community-at-large.

There is no doubt that this family was in trouble. The younger son not only has no sense of shame, but there is no evidence of any family or community loyalty. Through the village gossip network there is no doubt that the villagers were aware of what was taking place. The younger son's request and the elder son's receiving two-thirds of the inheritance, while remaining silent and not coming to the defense of his father, left the villagers dumbfounded. There must have been some feeling among the villagers to isolate this family lest the contagion spread. There is more here than an errant son. The well-being of a family and its extended family is at stake. George Shillington points out that even the family's ability to call upon the village in time of need is in jeopardy. If the family should lose its honor, no one would marry its sons and daughters, patrons would disappear, and the family would be excluded from necessary social and economic functions. "Families that do not maintain solidarity with neighbors are quickly in trouble" (*Jesus and His Parables*, p. 147).

The elder son is mentioned twice in this opening scene. In these opening verses we are given evidence that this family's dysfunction may be more widespread than first thought. In verse 12 we discover that the eldest son also received his share of the inheritance, which is two-thirds. You would expect him to loudly refuse it and come to the defense of his father. The fact that he remains silent suggests that his relationship with his father is not what it should be. In first-century Palestine, the listeners would not only expect him to refuse the inheritance, but, to be culturally correct, he should act as the third party reconciler. His silence means he was willing to accept his share and to refuse to be a mediator. The final result was the father "divided his property between them." The younger son now prepares to leave home while the elder son takes his share of the inheritance and remains at home.

The younger son gathers his things, bids his father and elder brother farewell, and with his inheritance in hand leaves. The father stands quietly at the entrance of the door and watches his son depart. He is not thinking at this point about his success, or if he will mature in a distant land. As an anxious father he is asking himself, "Will I ever see him again?" The son may be acting within his rights, but he is destroying his closest relationships in the process.

He is now free. Free from parental control. He travels down a distant road that will lead him to all the things he has wanted and where he will become what he has always wanted to be. It is the same road that sons and daughters have traveled for centuries.

There is nothing new about this story. It has been repeated ever since there have been parents and children. This young man was following the instincts of an uncontrollable, burning desire — to do what he wanted to do, when and how he wanted to do it. Unfortunately, we learn to demand our rights before we learn to value our relationships.

He was traveling into an illusionary, fanciful world of his own making. He wanted *liberty* without law, but there is no such liberty. He wanted *freedom* without restraint, but there is no such freedom. He wanted *life* without responsibility, but there is no such life. As he begins his journey to a distant land feeling now he is free, he fails to see that no one is free from the restrictions imposed by other people. No one is free from the restrictions imposed by their own personality. No one can be free from the restrictions imposed by God. We are always in bondage. The question is: "What bondage?"

For the father, this was no time for argument. After all, it would have been foolish to do so. So the father let him go. There was no last minute emotional plea on his part. Anyway, what kind of home would it be for a boy who did not want to be there? The father let him travel into a distant country to learn for himself, although he was tempted to give in to that natural, fatherly desire to protect his son from the pain and anguish of such an experience. Like every father, he wanted to shield his son from the inevitable consequences of a bad decision. But he resisted that desire — he let him go. It was the father's love that kept him from trying to keep his son home. It was a father's love that permitted him to let his son go and find his own life, even at the risk of losing it.

In this whole episode of the son's rebellion and departure, the father's pain was increased because the son was cutting himself loose from the way of living, thinking, and acting that had been handed down in this Jewish family from generation to generation as a sacred legacy. But this is one reason why the son is on the run, because this distant land is an appealing world where everything that was considered holy at home is disregarded.

Leaving home is much more than an historical event bound to time and space. Henri Nouwen states that "leaving home is a denial of the spiritual reality that I belong to God with every part of my being, that God holds me safe in an eternal embrace, that I am indeed carved in the palms of God's hands and hidden in their shadows. Leaving home means ignoring the truth that God has fashioned me in secret, moulded me in the depths of the earth and knitted me together in my mother's womb. Leaving home is living as though I do not yet have a home and must look far and wide to find one" (*The Return of the Prodigal*, p. 35). The psalmist in Psalm 139 discovered that even though he desired to flee from the presence of God, God will not go away. "Where can I go from your spirit? Or where can I flee from your presence?" (v. 7). He discovered that even though he would ascend to heaven, make his bed in Sheol, take the wings of the morning and dwell in the uttermost parts of the sea, "even there your hand shall lead me, and your right hand shall hold me fast" (v. 10). The prodigal, like Jonah, traveled to a distant land, and like Jonah, the further he traveled from the father's house the more intense the storm became.

For some, no matter their current success the sun is always shining brighter somewhere else. In the movie *Shadowlands*, C. S. Lewis described his life as living in shadowlands, like a person who always feels that the sun is shining brighter in the next valley or on a distant mountain. Like the prodigal there are those who are always on the move for a search that never ends. Why would the son leave a place where all he wanted to hear can be heard? Why would he ever want to leave a place where all he wanted to be he could become? Why? Because he did not believe it. It all sounds too unbelievable, even for us, that in our lost state to think that God comes to us like an elderly father nearly blind, stooped over by the weight of a lost son, standing in a dusty pathway, his heart scarred by the pain of rejection, waiting for the lost to return. This is exactly how God appears, so unexpected, so full of grace and love.

The son, clutching his inheritance, travels toward a distant land. From a distance, the "far country" can be very appealing. The younger son is acting within his rights, but he is destroying those roots that for so long have nurtured him, guided him, and have served him so well. In these early years it was these roots, these antecedents, that when the going got tough and his way unclear, gave him meaning and direction. Now he was willing to cast these roots to the wind, and follow his yearning for a distant land. Many times, a distant land looks more interesting in imagination than reality. But this seems to be something that one has to find out for one's self.

There are those haunting words of the hymn, "prone to leave the God I love." At this point of the parable, the episode of the son's leaving provides us with an accurate understanding of the parable. Quite possibly, it is the part of the parable that most of us identify with. It is at this point that we recognize the prodigal within each of us. Nouwen asks, "Why do I keep ignoring the place of true love and persist in looking for it elsewhere?" (p. 38). We fail to realize that the love we seek away from God in the world is a love that is based on "ifs." Such conditional love is based upon "if" you succeed, "if" you are intelligent, good-looking, and educated. The "ifs" enslave, because there is no way one can fully respond to such demands. Such worldly love remains slavishly conditional. Whereas, God's love, that we are prone to leave in our search in a distant land, is unconditional. God's unconditional love does not require that we prove anything. We are loved regardless of what or who we are. Yet the hymn writer is right, I am "prone to leave the God I love." We are plagued by an unsettling conviction *that happiness is always somewhere else*.

How can we explain such rebellion on our part? Some may see this as a reflection of Adam's original rebellion, as seen in our rejection of God in whose love we are created and by whose love we are sustained. Now the prodigal with his newly-found freedom leaves home. But he leaves home with a flawed freedom, a fictitious freedom that knows no fear, no reverence, and no limits. The fact remains that the unconditional love of God is a love that leaves us free to leave home, as well as, a love with outstretched arms that is willing to accept us back home again.

Discussion Questions

1. **Insensitive.** Is it possible that the desire to get, possess, and own is so strong that a person would wish the death of another person, even one's parent, in order to obtain it? How is it possible that a son could feel this way regarding his father? Have you ever desired anything that much? Have you ever experienced such insensitivity?

2. **Rebellion.** When the younger son left home he was cutting loose from the way of living, thinking, and acting that had been handed down to him for generations as a sacred legacy. Everything considered holy at home is disregarded. Have you ever struggled over the value of your own religious heritage? Does a religious heritage have any significance for today's generation?

3. **Responsibility.** Did you notice in the unfolding of the parable that the elder son received two-thirds of the inheritance? As the elder son, he is to be the protector and defender of his father. But regarding the harsh and unjust treatment of the father, he remains silent. Is this an indication that there is a breakdown between both sons and their father? Have you had moments when you remained silent, only to regret it later?

4. **Imagination.** Do you agree that a distant land looks more interesting in our imagination than in reality? Like the prodigal, does a person have to find this out for oneself? What has been your experience?

5. **Searching.** Why are we plagued by an unsettling conviction that happiness is always somewhere else? Consider Henri Nouwen's statement, "Why do I keep ignoring the place of true love and persist on looking for it elsewhere?" What has been the results of your personal searching?

Prayer

Today, O Lord,

    let me put right before interest;

    let me put others before self;

    let me put things of the spirit before the things of the body;

    let me put the attainment of noble ends above the enjoyment
        of present pleasures;

    let me put principle above reputation;

    let me put thee above all else.

O thou the reflection of whose transcendent glory did once appear unbroken in the face of Jesus Christ, give me today a heart like his — a brave heart, a true heart, a tender heart, a heart with great room in it, a heart fixed on thyself, for his name's sake. Amen.

— From *A Diary of Private Prayer*, John Baillie

Chapter Two

Confused, Alone, And Lost

"A few days later the younger son gathered all he had and traveled to a distant country, and there he squandered his property in dissolute living. When he spent everything, a famine took place throughout that country, and he began to be in need. So he went and hired himself out to one of the citizens of that country, who sent him to his fields to feed the pigs."   — Luke 15:13-15

Commentary

The text states, "The younger son gathered all he had and traveled to a distant country." George Shillington has pointed out that living in our contemporary, individualistic oriented society makes it difficult for us to understand this ancient Mediterranean family. "In peasant societies identity is thus family identity, not individual identity ... Family members are deeply embedded in each other socially, economically, and psychologically; hence the loyalty they owe to each other is simply categorical" (*Jesus and His Parables*, p. 145). Recognizing this solidarity is helpful to our understanding of the parable.

Next to the solidarity of the family is the solidarity of the community. For generations these families had lived in close proximity to one another. Their very survival depended on it. They faced the brutality of the ancient world together realizing that they could never survive alone. Over the course of many generations they had developed deep feelings and attachments for one another. They learned through their many years of experience that social conformity regarding village life was essential for survival. It was necessary to keep sharp boundaries between themselves and all others, between *we* and *they*. Shillington concludes, "Obviously *going into a distant country* where one was a stranger was not a very good idea" (p. 146). This was especially true regarding a greenhorn, inexperienced young man. It was like leading a sheep to the wolves.

The conflict in village life often is a result of conflict in the family, and family conflict usually centers around marriage and inheritance. (That has a contemporary ring to it.) The village considered family conflict as a serious matter if there was a possibility that land within the village would slip from family and village control into the hands of a stranger — God forbid a Gentile. "In such a setting, land claims are not written public records but a matter of collective memory. Thus breaking solidarity with the village could literally result in land claims being forgotten" (Shillington, p.146).

When the villagers realize the younger son is frantically running around the neighborhood trying desperately to sell his portion of the land and to turn it into cash as soon as possible, they naturally become fearful about the future of their village. The father's problem with his son has now become the community's problem. The actions of the younger son have now become a deep threat and concern of the entire village. Therefore, as the prodigal *traveled to a distant country* he is not only lost to his family but also a threat to the community (Bailey, p. 168). The loss of family property to a stranger was a very serious community problem.

Jeremias states that the Jewish Diaspora (the scattering of Jewish colonies outside of Palestine) had been estimated at four million in the first century, whereas the Jewish population in Palestine was estimated at about half a million at most. The Jews were drawn by the more favorable working conditions in the great mercantile cities in the Near East (*Rediscovering the Parables of Jesus*, p. 102). However, this was not the reason for the prodigal's leaving home. He was not pursuing a new business opportunity. He was not an entrepreneur seeking to establish a new business in a thriving Near Eastern city. He was a rebel on the run. MacLean Gilmour in his exegesis of this passage states that the phrase "he gathered all he had" suggests that by this time all of his possessions had been converted into cash so as to finance his journey.

"Traveled to a distant country" suggests to Jesus' hearers a journey into a Gentile country, possibly North Africa, Egypt, or Babylon (*Interpreter's Bible*, vol. 8, p. 272).

Scholars point out that there were a series of famines in and around Jerusalem from 169 B.C.E. to C.E. 70 (Jeremias, p. 104). Famine would have been a very powerful image for any first-century Palestine audience. A lone Jew in a far country without money and friends would have been especially vulnerable in a great famine. This seems to be expressed by the adding of the emphatic pronoun *he*, in verse 14 which reads, "He began to be in need." Understandably, *he*, more than others, was in need. A food shortage always hurts the poor and homeless first.

"Dissolute living" has been translated in varies ways, i.e. reckless, extravagant, and riotous living. Bailey in his desire to capture the original cultural meaning of the parable has discovered in his study of the Asian texts that the money was wasted and the terms to describe this wastefulness are indolence and recklessness. The texts do not label the prodigal as immoral, but extravagant and careless. He points out that the Greek text along with the Asian text do not condemn the prodigal for immorality (Bailey, p. 170), although at a later point in the story the charge of immorality is made by the elder son in verse 30.

After losing all he had and desperately attaching himself to a stern business man in a distant land, he was now about to lose his Jewishness. The hearers of the parable would have realized that his employment was the most degrading that a Jew could perform. They were very much aware of the biblical passages that forbid such behavior, i.e. Leviticus 11:7 and Deuteronomy 14:8. Jeremias points out that since he was in contact with unclean aminals he could not observe the sabbath, reducing him to the lowest depths of degradation and forcing him to deny his Hebrew heritage at every turn.

Verse 16 tells us how bad and desperate things had gotten: "He would have gladly filled himself with the pods that the pigs were eating; and no one gave him anything." Scholars have pointed out that only when Israel was reduced to such a state of poverty that they had to eat carob pods, then they repented of their evil ways. Maybe this is a subtle indication in the text that a new direction is about to take place in the prodigal's life. The Jews listening to the narrative knew this and could see a similarity between a wayward and disobedient Israel and a rebellious son. Bailey points out that carob is eaten and enjoyed by people of all ages all over the countryside of Palestine, Syria, and Lebanon even today. The carob has always been an edible and nourishing food in the Middle East. However, there were two varieties of carob pods. One variety contained a high level of sugar, and molasses was made from it. In the time of severe famine, it was hard to believe that it was fed to pigs. The other variety was a wild carob. It was more of a shrub and pigs could grub for its berries, which are bitter and lacking nourishment (Bailey, p. 172f). This variety of carob seems to fit the story in the parable.

Reflections

The young man makes his move and gradually descends into a hell of his own making. He was determined and persistent that he was going to leave home. He kicked over the restraints and the restrictions of his father's house. He said, "Good-bye," to his father and older brother and the words "gathering all he had and traveled" to a distant country bring to an end the son's relationship with his father. He was heading for the distant land of his dreams. There were pitfalls, dangers, and uncertainties lurking down that distant road, and he heard all about this from friends and family before he left, but he was convinced that there are some things a person just has to find out for himself.

He could not resist the lure of the forbidden and the unknown. Even though his friends tell him that the distant land is a forbidden land, the very thing forbidden becomes the thing desired. The very thing that he must not have becomes the thing to have. To tell a child not to touch something makes it the very thing to touch. Every time a book is banned for one reason or another, it becomes it the book to read. Book bannings have a way of producing bestsellers. Although many advised the prodigal about the foolishness of his decision and the folly of his journey into a far country, it all added to the lure and the attraction of that distant land. There is something exhilarating about the "call of the wild."

The young son is a rebel to the core. Not only does he do the unthinkable, ask for his inheritance before his father's death, but he compounds the problem created by his heartless offensive action against his father by selling everything and running away. So he takes the money and runs, never giving any thought about the pain and anguish that he leaves behind. At this point there was no turning back. For the first time he was living a life without restraint. There was no one around who was advising him regarding his behavior or his decisions. Now he was on his own. He was free and accountable to no one. However, freedom is never without restraints and he never understood these restraints or how his freedom was related to the family and to the folks back home.

He threw restraint to the wind. Arriving in that distant land, he discovered that he was now the center of attention. He spent freely. When he walked down the street, his new wardrobe, in the latest fashion, drew attention. His lavish apartment in the best part of town had class and it was the envy of many. He flashed his cash, and when he drank, everybody drank. Because he had so much to give, such generosity would always draw a crowd. For some people the only way to gain a friend is through their generosity. People will always come to share your money. As the story progresses, the son's situation deteriorates. The narrative is painting a picture of pending degradation and desperation. Recklessness ultimately begs a day of reckoning. Disregarding discipline, restraint, and responsibility in the name of freedom inevitably results in disappointment, confusion, and chaos. One morning he woke up — and it was all gone. He had "squandered his property in dissolute living." He spent everything he had. There was nothing left. He was confused, lost, and, worst of all, he was alone. Suddenly his whole world had fallen apart.

How could this young man get himself into such a situation? George Foster provides interesting insight into this first-century setting. He points out that peasants through history have admired the city. It holds a fascination like a candle for a moth. Since the beginning of time, city people have ridiculed, ignored, or exploited local country people upon whom they are dependent for food, taxes, labor, and market sales. Peasants need the city to buy their farm produce as well as providing for them products that they cannot produce themselves. "Yet the peasant recognizes that the city is the source of their helplessness and humiliation ... the peasant knows he can never really count on a city man" (*Peasant Society*, p. 10).

Consider what this freedom looks like outside of the father's house. It is not a pretty picture. In this newfound freedom in a distant land, what he does not want to be he now becomes — a slave. As a Jew, what he would never consider doing and would abhor doing, he now does — feed pigs. What he has never felt, what he never wanted to feel, he now feels — hunger. What he never wanted to be, he now is — alone. That is what freedom looks like outside of the father's house. It is reminiscent of the words of the apostle when he cried from the depth of his own despair, "Wretched man that I am! Who will rescue me from this body of death?" (Romans 7:24). Capon points out that "in a far county the rich boy turned into a lost cause. Whatever life he had is now over" (*Parables of Grace*, p. 138). Like so many runaway children in a strange land, he has lost the support base of his family. Without skill and training he is vulnerable to all the dangers and pitfalls that lurk in a foreign and strange land.

Now the break with his family is complete as he joins with a citizen in a strange land. In his desire to reestablish his well-being — he moves out of his own family and seeks to regain his dignity and pride in another tribe and people. The text states in a graphic way that the prodigal *glued* himself to a citizen of that country. His association with the owner was a desperate relationship that represented his only hope of survival. In the Asian culture a polite way a Middle Easterner gets rid of an unwanted hanger-on is to offer him a task that he knows the person will refuse. But to the surprise of the listener/reader, the citizen's attempt to get rid of the younger son fails. But if he thought his new associations were to be like his former life back home with his father, he is gravely mistaken. His need for food is so great and his situation so desperate, he accepts the job as a *feeder of pigs*. Young suggests perhaps the anti-Semitism of the Greco-Roman world is portrayed by the non-Jewish employer "when he sends the boy into the field to feed swine, knowing how offensive this would be to him" (*The Parables of Jesus*, p. 144). The situation was so desperate "he would gladly have filled himself with the pods that the pigs were eating, and no one gave him anything" (15:16). This could suggest that he tried his hand at begging and he failed even at that. When he cried, "But here I am dying of hunger," it strongly suggests that he was on the verge of starvation. Bailey concludes that the parable depicts a pig herder trying desperately to get enough nourishment to keep himself alive by eating black, bitter berries which the pigs root from the low shrubs that grow in the pastureland of the Middle East (p. 173). This young man was in dire straits and he needed to find a solution to his severe problem.

In drifting away from the father's house, he reached a level of despair that he never thought possible. The feeding of the swine was an unthinkable position for a Jewish boy. If he had been told years earlier that he would have done such a thing, his answer would have been, "No way possible that something like that could ever happen to me." He knew well the Talmudic proverb, "Cursed is the man who tends to swine, and the man who teaches his son Greek wisdom."

Even more disconcerting for him was the fact that he could not observe the sabbath and that along with his association with unclean animals, he was now forced to renounce the regular practice of his Jewish faith. Things seem to go from bad to worse. This fellow who never was subject to anyone but a loving father, now finds himself subject to a heartless, strange business man in a far country. His freedom comes to an abrupt end.

Desperate men do desperate things. He desired to get down with the pigs and eat the carob pods that they ate. In the first-century Middle East, the carob pods were eaten by the very poor who could find no other food. The prodigal could fill his stomach with them and never get his fill. This seems to depict the characterizing of the prodigal's life as being lost, confused, and alone as he tries to keep himself alive by eating the black, bitter berries which the pigs root from the carob shrubs. In his desperation he competes with the pigs for food. It has been suggested that in his eating like an animal he loses even his humanity to say nothing of his dignity. In a foreign land he is without money, food, family, tribe, or even humanity. Bernard Scott suggests that "this section of the narrative paints a story of disaster with verbs that describe the son's descent into despair, 'he began,' 'he was attached,' 'he longed,' and 'he desired' and as the story progresses the son's situation deteriorates" (p. 114). Not only is he experiencing the famine that has gripped the land, but he is suffering a famine of the heart which is expressed in his loneliness and desperation. It could be that the injection of the famine into the story, realizing that famine is the scourge of the ancient world, draws a sense of sympathy from the hearers of the parable to the son, for although he is responsible for his fate, he is not responsible for this downturn of nature which has worsened his plight.

In this pitiful condition the son had no further claim upon his father. He had received from his father all that he was entitled to. His older brother owed him nothing. Neither could he expect any help from his fellow townspeople. Bailey points out, if he returned to the village in such a condition he would receive nothing but taunts and outrage from the villagers, even possible physical abuse.

Instead of hearing the words of his father, he now hears the words of despair. What he was hearing were the desperate words that he kept saying over and over to himself, "No one gives me anything." "I am dying of hunger." In such a state, one can go on and say, "Life is not worth living," leading one to say, "I can't do anything right" and "I am worthless." This reveals how far he has traveled from the father's house. He has allowed the darkness of a distant land to absorb him so completely that now there is no light to turn toward. Helmut Thielicke suggests that this desperate son cries out, " 'I wanted to become myself. I thought that I would get all of this by cutting myself off from my father and my roots. Fool that I am. I have nothing but chains.' And a bitter laughter goes up from the pigsty" (*The Waiting Father*, p. 26).

As Jesus told this parable to those listeners in first-century Palestine, he had in mind the love of a heavenly Father who would never let this son go. The father's love followed him all the way into a distant land. It could be that Jesus was recalling the words of Psalm 139 where God is inescapable. The psalmist seems to understand the mind of a prodigal in that he knows within men and women there is a desire to escape from God. Paul Tillich states, "He who has never tried to flee from God, has never experienced the God who is" (*Shaking the Foundations*, p. 40). The psalmist talks about a God who knows all and sees all. Who can stand to have such a witness to one's life? Who can stand to be known in the darkest corners of one's soul? "You search out my path ... are acquainted with all my ways ... even before a word is on my tongue, O Lord, you know it completely" (vv. 3-4). The psalmist concludes that such knowledge is too much for him. This God even "discerns" his thoughts, thus his final way of escape, the most intimate of all his plans, is known by God. Tillich asks, "Who can stand to be known in such transparency? Fact is, we don't even wish to be known by ourselves" (p. 41). Like the prodigal, we want to flee to a place where God does not count anymore, at least for the present. Who doesn't want to flee from a companion who is at every turn of the road? Who doesn't want to break from a person of such perpetual companionship? The psalmist cried, "O Lord ... you hem me in, behind and before, and lay your hand upon me ... even the darkness is not dark to you ... you knit me in my mother's womb ... your eyes beheld my unformed substance" (vv. 5, 12, 13, 16). Thus, in light of Psalm 139, there is no ultimate isolation from God. The psalmist declared even when "I come to the end — I am still with you" (v. 18). He describes God as one who is greater than we are and has a claim upon us, not only because of creation, but also in re-creation, for God "leads me in the way everlasting" (v. 24). Tillich concludes, "He is God only *because* he is inescapable. And only that which is inescapable is God" (p. 40).

The prodigal is lost. He is not only lost but he is confused. His value system has been warped, he lacks a sense of direction, and his religious values have been severely compromised. In drifting so far from the presence of his father's house, he has reached a level of despair that he never thought possible. He is so lost, that it appears there is nothing else for him to do. Like Jonah, he ran as far as he could in the opposite direction. Sitting in a pigsty with his head in his hands, he could run no more. His pockets were empty, his stomach was empty, and he was suffering from a painfully empty, aching heart. In such a desolate condition, not even sin was any longer fun. It was the loss of everything that brought him to the bottom line of his identity. He had to hit the bedrock of his being before coming in touch with reality. The prodigal was not the first person to hit rock bottom before discovering the Rock of Ages.

Discussion Questions

1. **Dysfunctional.** In the prodigal's first-century peasant society, identity is family identity and not individual identity. The loyalty they owe and provide for each other is simply categorical. How did the prodigal break this solidarity? How did it lead to the family becoming dysfunctional? Did the son willfully break a commandment? Which one?

2. **Recklessness.** What about the phrase, "recklessness ultimately begs a day of reckoning"? Do you agree that disregard for discipline, restraint, and responsibility in the name of freedom results in disappointment, confusion, and chaos? Give some examples.

3. **Lost.** How could a young man with such a loving father get himself into such a lost and desperate situation? How desperate did he become? What things did he do that he thought he would never do? Have you ever been in such desperate despair? Did you ever do things you thought you would never do?

4. **Inescapable.** Do you think as Jesus told this parable, he had in mind Psalm 139 where God is seen as inescapable? Look at the words of that Psalm. How do they relate to a young man on the run? How have you experienced this inescapable love of God?

5. **Forbidden.** No doubt before he left, the younger son heard about the pitfalls, dangers, and uncertainties lurking down that distant road from friends and family. Why did he go? Why is there a lure and attraction to the forbidden? Why is it that the very thing forbidden becomes the thing desired? Is experience the best teacher?

Prayer

Grant, O God,
That we may never lose the way through our self will,
    and so end up in the far countries of the soul;
That we may never abandon the struggle
    but that we may endure to the end,
    and so be saved;
That we may never drop out of the race,
    but that we may ever press forward
    to the high goal of our calling;
That we may never choose the cheap and passing
    things, and let go the precious things
    that last forever;
That we may never take the easy way,
    and so leave the right way.
      — From *Prayers for the Christian Year*, William Barclay

Chapter Three

Homesickness

"But when he came to himself he said, 'How many of my father's hired servants have bread enough to eat and to spare, but here I am dying of hunger! I will get up and go to my father, and I will say to him, "Father, I have sinned against heaven and before you; I am no longer worthy to be called your son; treat me like one of your hired hands." ' "

— Luke 15:17-19

Commentary

There is a Jewish proverb that says, "When the Israelites stand in need of carob beans, then they return to God." There seems to be a correlation between the eating of the carob pod and the coming to repentance. This story regarding the use of the carob pod was known in Jesus' time (*The Parables of Jesus*, Brad Young, p. 145). Possibly, the use of carob pods in this story is an indication of what is about to take place. In the mind of the sages, poverty could lead the people into recognition of their need for God. Now that the son's situation is so bad that he desires to eat the carob pods that were fed to the pigs, then repentance is not that far away. In one verse he is starving and desiring the carob pods, and in the next verse "he came to himself."

When "he came to himself," he came to the reality of his situation — that he was starving to death. The pigs he was feeding were used for food for the business man who hired him. It was customary in the Middle East that when the owner butchered the pigs he would give the less desirable pieces to his hired help. Bailey points out that it is understandable that a Jew raised in a noble Jewish family would be unable to eat such food even if he was starving (p. 173). Nevertheless, the phrase "when he came to himself" is an indication that a change is about to take place and the prodigal is beginning to overcome his self-destructive behavior. For the first time he is taking a good look at himself. It is now obvious to him that he is a slave and he is starving. He who looked so much like his father now looks worse than any of his father's hired servants who at least have enough food to eat. "Coming to himself," suggests that the downward spiral to self-destruction is about to be reversed and his tragic lifestyle is about to change. Alan Culpepper states that there are three steps involved in the prodigal's return: 1) He comes to himself. 2) He arises. 3) He goes to his father (*New Interpreter's Bible*, vol. IX, p. 302). As he now begins to make his move homeward, he states that he is no longer worthy to request any of his father's goods and morally he has no right to be called his son.

Some scholars have been skeptical regarding the son's repentance (Scott, *Hear Then The Parables*, p. 116). Bailey suggests that the prodigal's plan that he intends to offer to his father when he arrives at home lacked repentance. He concludes, "With pride intact he intends to order his father to make him a hired servant" (p. 178). He is unwilling to cast himself on his father's mercy and grace. But Jeremias presents a strong case when he points out that the phrase "he came to himself" is an expression of repentance in Hebrew and Aramaic (p. 102). "In coming to himself" the son realizes his responsibility for his wrongdoing. He wants to make the matter right. Although his repentance may appear to be made on his own need for food and he seems to view his father as a bank manager rather than a loving father, he does, however, express a sense of shame: "I have sinned." He seems to recognize that the sin that he has committed was against God (*against heaven*) and his father (*against you*). In owning up to the sins that he committed against God and his father, he makes it clear that he is repenting for the terrible wrong that he has done. Many commentators point out that the parable recalls the rich terminology of Hebrew imagery. Young states, "Without a doubt, the expression 'he came to himself' is best understood as the Hebrew or Aramaic terminology for repentance. The essence of repentance in Jewish thought means to come home ... He had done serious wrong. While he broke the commandments, his greatest sin is his broken relationship with his father, the cause of all the wrong in his life. He must go back home and make matters right with his father" (p. 147).

Reflections

"When he came to himself," he was now doing some serious thinking. Reason and honesty were now about to take hold of his thinking. What finally brought him to this place? *First*, he became fully aware of how lost he was when no one in his surroundings paid any attention to him. They noticed him while he had something they could use, but when he had no money left to spend and no gifts to give, he stopped existing for them. He finally realized he was utterly alone, a complete stranger in a foreign land, and if he did not get some assistance soon he was not going to make it. *Second*, when no one offered him the food that they were bringing to feed the pigs, he then realized how disconnnected he was from life — from family, friends, country, acquaintances, and even food. *Third*, Henry Nouwen points out, when the prodigal was being treated like a pig and found himself eating with them and living with them, it was then that he came in touch with his ground of being — realizing he was no pig, but a human being, a son of the father (Nouwen, *The Return of the Prodigal*, p. 44). After coming to the doorstep of starvation and death — *he came to himself.* Now he begins to remember. His memory literally will save him and bring him back from the abyss.

Bill Glass, an All-Pro defensive lineman for twelve years with the Cleveland Browns, tells about his prison ministry that took place in more than 100 prisons across the United States in his book *Crime: Our Second Vietnam*. He said he learned something about everyday life as he visited men on death row. At the Mississippi State Prison, he met with 44 men on death row and asked them, "How did you get along with your daddy?" He said he got 44 answers: "I hated my dad!" Glass said, "I learned never to turn my back on a man who hates his father." He is convinced that a major cause of crime is a result of a son's bad relations with his father.

Glass asked the head of the Florida State Prison system, "How many Jews are there in your prison system?" He replied, "Thirty-three." As Glass pondered the question why there are so few Jews in prison, he said he thought he possibly knew the answer. For centuries Jewish fathers have blessed their sons at age thirteen. Glass concludes, "This carries over to the rest of their lives — you don't see many Jews in prison" (p. 79). He told the story regarding Kirk Douglas who was interviewed on television about his new book, *The Ragman's Son*, his life story. The interviewer asked him, "What do you miss the most in your life?" "Being blessed by my father," he said. He said his father traveled the streets of Philadelphia selling rags, but he never blessed him. This famous film star, before a television audience, with tears streaming down his face at 75 years of age, tells the world that he was never able to please his father and receive his blessing. Glass points out that mothers seem to give their blessing better than fathers. He said if you don't think so, watch a football game on television. Invariably the players comments are "Hi, Mom!" and sometimes "I love you." Glass believes that mothers seem to give their blessing more easily and naturally to their children than their fathers, and the men on death row have problems with their fathers and it makes them mean.

The prodigal had his father's blessing and it saved his life. Whatever this young man lost in a distant land — money, friends, reputation, self-respect — he still remembered his father and his blessing, his home, and his heritage. If he was not loved and blessed by his father, he would have resented and cursed his father, blaming his father for his failure. He never did. He never resented his father; in fact, when he came to his senses, his first thoughts were, "I will arise and go to my father." Most sons and daughters who run from home do so because they are in search of love, value, and belonging. They never received their father's blessing. This is one of the reasons for the popularity of gangs in our urban communities, because gangs give youth both a sense of belonging and a sense of family. The prodigal never found a lasting relationship in a distant land because he knew he had one at his father's house. What made life so dissatisfying in this distant land was knowing about the life he had had earlier. Even in his state of confusion and being lost, he could not forget how it was back home. He could not erase from his mind his earlier life. Although he was now a nobody in a distant land, he remembered the days when he was somebody in the father's house. He could not forget who he was. In fact, it was the memory of what he had left that helped him to understand what he must do.

Hendrick Kraemer was a Dutch theologian who lived in the Netherlands during the Second World War. A group of Christians came to him in 1939 and said, "Dr. Kraemer, we are deeply disturbed. Some of our Jewish friends have disappeared and we do not know what has happened to them. We do not know what to do. Could you tell us what to do?" The theologian responded, "I cannot tell you what to do. I can tell you who you are. If you remember who you are, you will know what to do." They thanked him and went out and organized the Dutch Resistance Movement. The prodigal could not forget who he was. He was the son of a loving and caring father.

He is now remembering his own past and thereby remembering who he is. It is a moment of self-recognition. It is a moment of recognition of his family from which he derives his identity. This is one of those hopeful moments for anyone who has lost their way. Shillington suggests that although the prodigal is a long way from being with his father, yet his memory connects him with the family's social networkings and places him in a social consciousness in which he knows how he should operate. Perhaps this will bring the insight and guidance for which he is searching in his desperate desire to answer his own question, "What am I going to do now?"

His memory caused a homesickness that literally saved his life. It was the fact that he did remember a time when things were much better for him that saved him from his despair. His homesickness saved him in that he never became a citizen of that distant land. He never felt at home. He never forgot that there was a better life, a different life, a far more meaningful life. He remembered that his father had hired servants at home who were much better off than he was. They had bread and he was starving to death.

What made this whole experience so painful for him was the fact that he did not have to be in this position. He knew it was all self-inflicted and he had brought this upon himself. But the hardest thing for him to admit was that he was wrong, that he made the wrong choices and followed the wrong impulses. He now had to be realistic about his plight, but facing the realism of the situation was difficult. There was the feeling that if he hung on for a little while longer, it might all turn out all right. But realism stared him in the face. He had his freedom, but he knew it was tarnished. He had his inheritance, but now it was gone. He had his freedom, but it had turned into the worst kind of bondage — a bondage that had bound him to a citizen of a far country resulting in the loss of his Jewishness and self-respect.

He knew he could not blame his situation on somebody else. He could not blame his father, his brother, or his neighbors. He knew this was the result of his own actions, his own decisions, and his own ambitions. This made his homesickness all that more acute. Although he had acquired what he so desperately felt he needed, his inheritance and his freedom to do as he pleased, yet his acute sense of lostness came from what he did not have — the assurance of his father's love and acceptance. This is one thing that every young man craves. In this distant land friendship, relationship, and intimacy began to take on new meanings.

In the biblical setting, the wilderness experience seems to have a cathartic effect. It was in a "desert of despair" that Moses heard the call of God. It was also in this desert experience that he was aware of his own limitations and inadequacies. He became acutely aware of his own vulnerability, and any notions regarding his independence were put to rest. It was in the desert that the children of Israel wandered for forty years until an entire generation had died off — certain ways of thinking had to be purged. Only after they had experienced this "desert of despair" gaining a sense of their identity and mission could they make their move toward the promised land. For the prodigal this "desert of despair" was a painful experience, but through this anguish he made remarkable discoveries about himself. It was here that he discovered the truth about his illusions, his vulnerability, his limitations. Here he discovered the value of relationships and intimacy. Kenneth G. Pfifer in his *Book of Uncommon Prayer* prays:

> *Yet, O Lord, the very things I handle and see lose meaning when they become ends in themselves.... If I avoid love, diminish hope, deny faith, my appreciation of my house and land, my meat and potatoes shrinks, and I become a little man with little aims and little power.*

This was the struggle that the prodigal had gone through — things had become ends in themselves.

It would be a terrible thing if we could feel right when we have done the wrong thing. In his homesickness, he was suffering the torment of a wrong decision. Even though he got what he wanted, he knew it was not right. It never felt right. He tried to convince himself that it was right, but he was never really able to do so. In the popular movie, *Wall Street*, a young stockbroker (played by Charlie Sheen) has a tremendous drive to become a success on Wall Street. He meets a real shaker and mover in a rather ruthless Wall Street broker (played by Michael Douglas), who says the memorable line, "What is important is greed. Greed has made this country great!" This ruthless tycoon becomes the young stockbroker's mentor. He begins to act, dress, and think like him. Then the young man comes to himself and suddenly realizes that the person he is becoming is not the person he wants to be. He changes his life before irreversible disaster sets in.

In our narrative, the young prodigal begins to see that the person he is becoming is not the person he wants to be. I can remember as a young boy I asked my mother for money to buy an ice cream cone. She refused to give it to me. When she was not looking, I went to her purse and took the money and made my way to the ice cream store and got my ice cream. It was the most awful-tasting ice cream I had ever eaten. It was not enjoyable and I ended up throwing it away. My conscience would not let me forget the devious and underhanded means I had used to procure it. What I expected to be an enjoyable experience was miserable. The worst part was yet to come — I had to tell my mother and work to replace the money.

The homesickness was intensified by the prodigal's knowledge that the pressure he brought against his father to secure his inheritance must have hurt his father deeply. This was something that a decent, thoughtful, loving Jewish son would never request of his father. What made it all the more painful for him was his father's willingness to hand it all over to him without telling his son how deeply he had been hurt. The son could not run away from the fact that what he did and what he accomplished was at the expense of someone else's feelings and pain. He had what he wanted. He did things the way he wanted to do them — but the fulfillment of it all was missing, because he knew down deep he had used his father to accomplish his own selfish purposes. I agree: it would be a terrible thing if we could feel right when we have done wrong. There is nothing more futile than to know we have done wrong and then to try, against all odds, to convince ourselves that we have done right.

The prodigal had a feeling of disgust. However, Thielicke points out that merely being disgusted with himself was of no help. All that could do was make him a nihilist, but that would in no case show him the way home. In fact, it was the other way around. It was his thoughts about his father and his father's house that made him disgusted with himself. It was not because he was sick of the far country; his thoughts and memory about his father and his home made him disgusted with the far country. The fact is, he could never forget who he was.

What is the prodigal to do? He does not like what he has become. He cannot stand to be alone with his conscience. Down deep he knows the reason for his plight, but he cannot bring himself to admit and confess his own failure and sin. At this point he is struggling to take ownership of the consequences resulting from his poor decisions. What is he to do? I am reminded of the contrast between Judas and Peter. They both had committed the same sin — they denied Christ. Why Judas did what he did I am not sure. Obviously, he lost sight of a loving and all-forgiving God. After his betrayal, there could have been a homecoming, but it never happened. Jesus wanted a homecoming, but Judas took things into his own hands and according to Acts he plunged to his death. Jesus wanted a homecoming, but Judas never came. Peter also denied Christ, in fact, three times. In the midst of his remorse and sadness, he claimed his sonship. He returned in tears to a homecoming. Whereas Judas threw himself headlong down a precipice and took his own life, Peter threw himself on the mercy and grace of God, finding both forgiveness and new life. The prodigal faced a tough decision. Was he to trust his own impulses, feeling he could pick himself up and shake off the dust of this distant land, and by his newfound freedom start all over again by himself? Or was he going to throw himself on the mercy and grace of a loving father and trust everything to his father's willingness to accept and forgive him? Walter Brueggemann observes, "The promise of forgiveness is available, but it cuts deeply against the values that seem operative among the children of modernity." In other words, forgiveness yields a freedom to begin again, a freedom we crave and at the same time a freedom we dread.

The words, "but when he came to himself," suggest to the hearer that a fundamental change is about to take place in the story's direction and that a new day is about to dawn. Up to this time there is no doubt that the son's wilderness was of his own making. He was coming to realize he was suffering from the consequences of his own choice. Here in this lonely, isolated, strange, and foreign place he started to think rationally and honestly. It has been pointed out that the phrase, "when he came to himself," is a Greek medical term meaning "to come to one's senses after fainting." It is as though the prodigal had been asleep, out of touch with reality, and now he was regaining his consciousness and suddenly wakes up to the real world, saying to himself, "What on earth am I doing in a place like this? I belong in my father's house where even the hired servants are far better off than I am." He finally declares what he could not declare up to this point, "What a fool I have been." He realizes that if he returns, he will be put on the periphery of his family, since he has seemed to gain some sense of the magnitude of his deed. Nonetheless, he seems to feel even in this limited association he will be in a social location in which he knows how to operate that is so different from his present situation where he is totally dysfunctional. Even if he is not in full membership of the family, even possibly a hired servant, he will be restored. But most importantly, he will not be among strangers and outsiders who exploit, ridicule, and even ignore him. At this point, that is enough to give him a glimmer of hope. The prodigal was shut up in the loneliness and pain of a far country where he had no friends and no real joy nor inner peace. He had fallen so far in his life that he had more in common with pigs than people. This is what it took for him to come to himself. God has his own purposes when he leads us into the wilderness. One now has the feeling that the downward spiral of this tragic life is about to be reversed.

One of the most compelling factors that supported the prodigal through this entire ordeal was the fact that "he is still his father's son." Regardless that he had lost his self-respect, his pride, and his dignity, "he is still his father's son." No matter how far he had traveled into a distant land, "he is still his father's son." Although he has become so vile and unclean that he can no longer participate in the religious celebrations and practices that had nurtured him as a child and young man, "he is still his father's son." Although his physical appearance has been so altered by his lifestyle, his appearance would never give anyone the slightest indication that he once belonged to his father, yet "he is still his father's son." There is no land so distant, no sin so degrading, no rebellion so strong or defiant as to erase the fact that "he is still his father's son." Every son and daughter who has lost touch with the original goodness, forgetting that God has created every man and woman in his own image and that God's response was, "It is very good," needs to be reminded that despite all the dark voices, no one can ever change that. Nouwen discovers "that dark voices drown out that gentle, soft, light-giving voice that keeps calling me 'my favorite one'; they drag me to the periphery of my existence and make me doubt that there is a loving God waiting for me at the very center of my being" (p. 46). With the words, "when he came to himself," it now appears that the prodigal is beginning to discover that God-given light at the center of his being. Who of us has not experienced those dark voices that seek to lead us to the periphery of our existence? But when we come to our senses we realize God is waiting for us at the very center of our being.

Discussion Questions

1. **Change.** It now appears that the downward spiral to self-destruction is about to be reversed and the prodigal's tragic lifestyle is about to change. What has had to take place to bring him to this point? What similar experiences have you had?

2. **Memory.** When the younger son hit rock bottom, it was his memory that literally saved him. He remembered that he was still a son of his father. How critical is it in a state of being lost and alone to remember that there is a loving and caring God standing nearby? What things do you need to remember about the past that brings hope for the present and future? How does the sacrament of Holy Communion help us to remember? Why is that important?

3. **Blessing.** The prodigal never seemed to forget his father's blessing. The father's blessing has always been a very important aspect in Jewish family life. Do you believe the reason the prodigal never found a lasting relationship in a distant land resulted from his knowing that he had one at his father's house? Was it the memory of what he had left behind that helped him to understand what he must do? Have you ever had such moments of self-recognition? Explain.

4. **Confession.** Confession was long-coming for the younger son. Why is confession so difficult? Why do people complain regarding a prayer of confession during worship? Isn't it true that we would rather blame others than confess our wrongdoing? Do you find it difficult confessing that you have made the wrong choice and followed the wrong impulse? What benefits have you experienced through confession?

5. **Discovery.** It was in the painful experience in a distant land that the prodigal discovered the truth about his illusion, his vulnerability, and his relationships. What experiences have you had where you discovered the value of relationships and intimacy?

Prayer

Lord who has formed me out of the mud,
and hast redeem'd me through thy blood,
And sanctifi'd me to do good:

Purge all my sins done heretofore,
For I confess my heavy score,
And I will strive to sin no more.

Enrich my heart, mouth, hands in me,
With faith, with hope, with charity;
That I may run, rise, rest with thee.
         — George Herbert (*Classics of Western Spirituality* Series)

Chapter Four

The Turning Point

"I will get up and go to my father, and I will say to him, 'Father, I have sinned against heaven and before you; I am no longer worthy to be called your son; treat me like one of your hired hands.' " — Luke 15:18-19

Commentary

There is no doubt that the prodigal is at the end of his tether. As a Jew he has disgraced himself by becoming a swine herder. The plan that he devises seems to lack grace resulting from his genuine desire to repent. In his plan he intends to work and thereby fulfill his responsibility to his father. His request to be a hired servant is on his terms. He is telling his father what to do and orders his father to do it. If he is a servant standing before his master, then his plan is adequate. But since he is a son standing before a compassionate father, his plan is inadequate. At this point he has no idea that the restoration of this broken relationship will only result from his willingness to throw himself on the mercy of his father's grace. What he is really doing is seeking to soften his father's heart and then to offer his solution to the problem. Capon suggests that he is hoping "the old man is senile enough to make a deal" (*The Parables of Grace*, p.138). Regardless how one looks at it, his solution does not involve grace.

There is a repentance, but it is a self-serving repentance that offers the possibility of survival on the son's terms. Nouwen states:

> *I know this state of mind and heart well. It is like saying, "Well, I couldn't make it on my own, I have to acknowledge that God is the only resource left for me. I will go to God and ask for forgiveness in the hope that I will receive the minimal punishment and be allowed*

> *to survive on the condition of hard labor." God re-*
> *mains harsh and judgmental. Submission to this kind*
> *of God does not create true inner freedom, but breeds*
> *only bitterness and resentment.*
> — *The Return of the Prodigal*, p. 46

I am well aware that there are several factors that call into question the nature of the son's repentance. He has lost his sonship, his inheritance, and he has abrogated his Judaism, his religion. Because of his actions, what belonged to the family and in a sense to the community now belongs to foreigners. His statement, "make me one of your hired servants," suggests that his relationship with his father is dead as far as a son is concerned. The reclaiming of sonship seems to be out of the question for him because of the gravity of his sin against his father. Capon suggests that he has, by his prodigality, lost all claim to his former status as his father's loyal child. By the proposition that he wants to present to his father he is seeking to carve out a new life for himself (p. 138).

He works on his speech because he is not sure how his father will receive him. He has some very practical needs, such as food and money, and feeling that he has lost his sonship forever, he wants to negotiate to see if he can be a hired servant. After forfeiting his sonship, he will plead with his father to put him on the payroll. Oesterley points out that there are three levels of servanthood on the first-century Jewish estate (*The Gospel Parables in Light of Their Jewish Background*, p. 186). The bondsman (*paides*) was at the top of the staff of servants. He was a slave with servile status, yet he was regarded as part of the master's family and had a special interest in the affairs of the family. The bondservant (*douloi*) was one step lower than the bondsman. The lowest category was the servants (*misthioi*). They were neither part of the family nor did they have any interest in the affairs of the family. They were employed when there was work to be done and could be dismissed at the pleasure of the master. Although a free man, the servant had no rights or security. In essence, the prodigal was requesting that his father give him the lowest position of all — anything to be home. Granted that the envisioned return will only put him on the periphery of the family; nonetheless, it will reconnect him with the family's social network. Even though he is not in the full membership of the family, he will be in a social location in which he will know how to perform and will no longer be an outsider without acquaintance and food. Under the circumstances, that is enough to provide him with a sense of hope.

As a hired servant, he would be a free man with his own income living independently in the local village. This plan would make it possible for him to maintain his pride and his independence. As a hired servant, his thoughts may have been that he could work and fulfill his moral responsibility to his father. By paying back the squandered money, he hoped to make up his losses to his father, and thus earn his way back. Also, if he is a hired servant living off the premises, then he will not be eating his brother's bread (Bailey, p. 177). He knows now that everything left in the estate will be signed over to his brother, and by not living at home he will not have to reconcile with his brother. With all of these elaborate plans in place, he begins his journey home, but little did he know about the grace that waited him on his return.

Reflections

The prodigal now begins to compare his lot with that of his father's day laborers, to whom their kind master gives more bread than they can eat. Things do not stop there. Reality begins to settle in. He realizes how he has sinned against heaven and his father by his licentious life. He realizes that his sin against his father is of such magnitude that he is no longer worthy to be treated like his father's son.

After the prophet Isaiah had walked through the crowded city at festival time, watching the people as they hurried from one amusement to another only to come away with tired expressions and empty hearts, he then wrote, "Why do you spend your money for that which is not bread, and labor for that which does not satisfy?" (Isaiah 55:2). The question has been asked: Was the prodigal searching for adventure in a distant land where he could live without restraint and accountability, or was he searching for relationships and intimacy — seeking to love and be loved.

The story is told about Karl Valentine, the German comedian, who is standing alone on stage as the curtain goes up. The entire stage is dark except for a solitary circle of light that has been created by the street lamp. Valentine, with a deeply worried look on his face, walks around and around under the light desperately looking for something. A policeman enters the scene and asks, "What are you looking for?" "My house keys," Valentine answers. The policeman joins the search and together they search for the keys. After several moments of searching and finding nothing the policeman asks, "Are you sure you lost them here?" "No!" Valentine answers. Pointing to the darkness he states, "I lost them over there." "Then why on earth are you looking for them over here?" the policeman replied. Valentine's response was, "Because there is no light over there." The prodigal's search for an unconditional love had taken him to a distant land where it could not be found. How many times in our search for happiness do we go to extremes in order to find it? The extremes, such as money, sex, and power, drive us further from both our heart's desire and the father's house. Nouwen has it right when he states, "I am the prodigal son every time I search for unconditional love where it cannot be found. Why do I keep ignoring the place of true love and persist in looking for it elsewhere?" (p. 39).

If the son's search was for love, it could be that his love was marred by jealousy, scarred by envy, and limited by selfishness. But yet the prodigal still may have remembered the love that he had experienced in the father's house. For the prodigal there were those unforgettable moments in the father's house when he experienced forgiveness, generously and freely. He may have remembered those times when he crept home when he was bruised and hurt and was reassured that someone cared. Now, as he is about to creep home once more, he is hoping that forgiveness and acceptance would happen again. Carlo Caretto points out that love makes demands of us. It will question us from within. It will disturb us. Sadden us. Play havoc with our feelings. Reveal our superficialities. We hope, at last it will bring us to the light. We hope it will bring the prodigal sensibility. This verse from Charles Wesley's hymn speaks to his condition:

> *Come, Lord, and tame the tiger's force,*
> *Arrest the whirlwind in my will,*
> *Turn back the torrent's rapid course,*
> *And bid the headlong sun stand still,*
> *The rock dissolve, the mountain move,*
> *And melt my hatred into love.*

Sitting next to the hog trough, he takes a hard look at his life and finds nothing. This comparison allows him to realize how empty his life has become. Now the whole story takes on a different direction in light of the prodigal's self-discovery. Now he acknowledges he has sinned against heaven and his father. What was his sin against his father? His failure to hold himself in readiness to care for his father in his old age. He is now aware that loss of the money had a moral responsibility attached to it. What was his sin against heaven and God? His failure to keep the responsibility that the inheritance required of him. Also he broke one of the most important and revered laws of the Hebrew community — the fifth commandment.

But the cure for the sickness of his soul was now at hand. Leslie Weatherhead's statement is a valid one, "The forgiveness of sins is the most therapeutic thing in the world" (*Psychology, Religion and Healing*, p. 334). Repentance and confession could be the integrating factors that the son has been searching for. James Fenhagen talks about those moments when he is conscious that his life is in tune with God and the Spirit moves within him. He finds at times the sound is discordant, even harsh, but it remains one sound. There is a wholeness, even when the sounds are those of joy and pain — yet it remains a single unified sound. He confesses that there are those moments when the many-faceted aspects of his personality are playing in opposition to each other. "When this happens, I experience inner chaos and confusion, the very opposite of wholeness. The answer is not to play louder, not to pretend we do not hear, but rather to take time to listen to the many sounds so that the message they contain can be brought to light" (*Invitation to Holiness*, p. 62). For so long the prodigal seemed to want to play the discordant tune louder, while all the time adding to his chaos and confusion. Regardless of how difficult repentance and confession seemed to be, he is on the verge of discovering how they will lead to the integration, harmony, and wholeness of life.

One of the greatest challenges of the spiritual life is to receive God's forgiveness. Nouwen points out that we are hesitant to allow God to erase our past. It is as though we want to prove to God that our sins are just too great to be forgiven. Even though God wants to restore our relationship, we insist on being merely a hired servant. "Receiving forgiveness requires a total willingness to let God be God and do all the healing, restoring, and renewing. As long as I want to do even a part of that myself, I end up with partial solutions, such as becoming a hired servant" (p. 138).

Church members on numerous occasions have complained to me about the inclusion of a prayer of confession in the order of worship for the congregation to recite in unison. The reason for their objection is that it makes some people feel bad and talking about our offenses, sins, shortcomings, and negligence causes them to have a low esteem of themselves. They remind me that people come to church to feel better, not to feel worse. However, Christian confession is a means of grace. Because of our assurance of God's love, forgiveness, and acceptance, we can pick up from here and move on. Freed from the burden of guilt, we can now live with our real, sinful selves, accepting ourselves because God accepts us and forgives us. How liberating it is to pray this eucharistic prayer of confession.

> *Merciful God, we confess that we have not loved you with our whole heart. We have not done your will, we have broken your law, we have rebelled against your will, we have not heard the cry of the needy. Forgive us, we pray. Free us for joyful obedience, through Jesus Christ our Lord. Amen.*
> — *United Methodist Book of Worship*

I cannot think of anything that would make people feel better about themselves and boost self-esteem than to take part in a *prayer of confession* and the *words of assurance*. The prayer of confession was going to do wonders for the prodigal by helping him face the reality of his situation and see himself as he really was. Every desire to return to the father's house begins with an honest prayer of repentance.

When he said, "I will get up and go to my father, and I will say to him, Father I have sinned ..." it was as though all of the miles between him and his father at that moment had melted away. He was seeking guidance. He knew to whom he was to go. From this moment on, his life was to take a different direction. The decision to leave for a distant land caused fragmentation — creating a downward spiral resulting in his life coming apart. The decision to rise and go to his father was the beginning of an upward spiral — resulting in his life coming together. Now he was able to do something he could not previously do: he admitted his guilt and assumed his responsibilities outright.

It appears that the son's prayer, "Father, I have sinned against heaven and before you," is evidence of serious repentance on the son's part. Interpreting the Aramaic literally suggests reconsidering, changing one's opinion, and sorrowing for one's action. At this point in the text he offers no excuse. He repents, which leads him to confess that he had sinned against heaven and his father — meaning that he had not cared for his father in his old age and failed to keep the law. The rabbinic idea of repentance was not a work that a person did to earn God's favor, but rather for repentance to be seen as sincere, it needed to be accompanied by reparations for the sin committed along with a determination to avoid all further sin.

It has been suggested that the son, in the scheme of things, is commanding his father. He has a plan and he is expecting his father to carry out his plan. He feels it is worthy of execution. He may be suggesting to his father to disregard the past and implying that he is sorry for what he has done and that he is not totally useless to his father. One has the feeling that up to this point he is sorry only for the money he has lost and not for any pain that he may have caused his father. The son's plan to become one of the hired servants has several advantages for him. For one thing, he will be able to keep his independence, which would provide him the opportunity to compensate his father for his errors and possibly pay restitution. On his own terms and with his pride intact, he seeks to order his father to take him back as a hired servant. By this plan, he will save himself and reconciliation with his brother will not be necessary.

A grave shortsightedness on the son's part is his failure to consider the village's response to his return. The fact is that no one sins in isolation. What we do, for good or bad, has an effect on others. Many times we try to convince ourselves that our sins and misdeeds hurt only ourselves and no one else. How foolish for us to think that there are such a things as victimless misdeeds and sins. Our sins and misbehavior are always painful for those who love us. The prodigal may have thought that his actions were victimless; he failed to realize it brought deep pain to his father's heart and disgrace to his village. David Buttrick asks the question: How do we humans sin? His answer is: we sin in our corporate, social, and family identities. "Sin cannot be defined in terms of a personally motivated individual acting alone; we do most of our damage corporately" (*The Mystery and the Passion,* p. 103). How easily we can become like the prodigal, so unconscious, so unaware of the effects of our actions and words upon others.

Now, the question for the prodigal is: How is he going to face the hometown folks? It will be hard for him to gain any status in the village since he has failed in a distant country. In this cultural setting, it is going to be difficult for him to return after he has emigrated to a distant land. He offended the entire community by taking and losing his father's inheritance while his father was still alive. The villagers are offended because they are concerned what other villages will think of them and that they may be judged by the actions of this one villager. The village's pent-up hostility will be vented on him for having insulted his father, sold his land, and lost his inheritance to a Gentile. He does not seem to have any solution for this problem and he will simply have to face the villagers. For now he seems to have a three-point plan: to live in the village as a hired servant, fulfill his responsibility to his father, and face the mockery of the villagers. *He will do it because he is hungry.*

One thing we need to remember, when the prodigal made his confession and said, "I will get up and go to my father," he was beginning a journey. Maybe his motives were wrong, but at least he was headed in the right direction. Many times at the beginning of a journey our vision is impaired and our motives are suspect, just like Pilgrim in *Pilgrim's Progress*. But as the journey continues, our vision becomes clearer and we are more aware of our motives. Maturity and wisdom set in — there is a growing in grace. It is possible as the journey continues our values change with a broadening of our understanding of ourselves and the nature of our journey causing things to take a different direction. New values and goals resulting from the journey could possibly bring about a course correction, especially in regard to motives and purposes. This is what happened to the prodigal: he had a course correction along the way. During the course of the journey he got a glimpse of what a wretched person he really was. This self-understanding and awareness helped immensely to bring about the healing of his broken relationship with his father. The most important thing is to begin the journey home even though our vision is impaired and motives suspect — and to say, "I will get up and go to my father." He may have been motivated by the wrong purposes, but how many people come to church to worship and pray for the wrong reasons? But in the process their lives may be transformed. That is the power of the redemptive fellowship. We hope there will be healing along the way for the prodigal.

When the prodigal declared, "I will rise and go to my father," this marked the turning point in his life. For the first time he had a sense of direction. He knew what he must do. He set out to do it. Sue Monk Kidd calls this "the grateful center" (*God's Joyful Surprise*, p. 200). The prodigal had now acquired such a center in his life. There was no doubt as to where he must go, what he must do, and what he must say.

For the first time he was being directed by moral principle rather than lustful and selfish desires. He knew what he had to do even though he knew it would be painful. Reconciliation is never easy. Now, he knew what was required of him. Now he had direction. For the first time, he felt his life was on the right track. He begins the long, hard journey back to the father's house.

Discussion Questions

1. **Doubt.** The reclaiming of his sonship seems out of reach to the prodigal because of the gravity of his sin. He doubts his acceptance. He develops a plan and a prayer to make himself acceptable to his father. Where is grace in his proposition? What role has grace played in your relationship with God?

2. **Forgiveness.** One of the greatest challenges of the spiritual life is to receive God's forgiveness. Nouwen points out that we are hesitant to allow God to erase our past and we insist on being merely a hired servant. What must we do to allow God's forgiveness to bring the healing, restoring, and renewing that God intends for us?

3. **Influence.** As the prodigal prepares to go home, he has no idea of what the village's response will be regarding his return. Why was the village so concerned regarding the son's rebellion and the family's problems? What is the meaning of the statement, "No one sins in isolation"? What influence is your life having on others?

4. **Motives.** No doubt as the prodigal heads home, he is doing so with wrong motives, but he is heading in the right direction. Along the way there is a course correction resulting in true repentance and confession. How many people come to church for the wrong reasons, but are transformed along the way? Have you had a course correction along the way, resulting in wholeness and healing? Explain.

5. **Principle.** As the prodigal continues his journey toward his father's house, he has no doubt what he must do, where he must go, and what he must say. For the first time he is being guided by an inner moral principle rather than greed, lust, and selfish desires. Have you acquired a sense of moral direction in your journey?

Prayer

I want a principle within of watchful godly fear,
A sensibility of sin, a pain to feel it near.
I want the first approach to feel of pride or wrong desire,
To catch the wondering of my will,
And quench the kindling fire.

Almighty God of truth and love, to me thy power impart;
The mountain from my soul remove,
The hardness from my heart.
O may the least omission pain my reawakened soul,
And drive me to that blood again, which makes the wounded whole.
— Charles Wesley in *The United Methodist Hymnal*

Chapter Five

Homecoming

"So he set off and went to his father. But while he was still far off, his father saw him and was filled with compassion; he ran and put his arms around him and kissed him. Then the son said to him, 'Father I have sinned against heaven and before you; I am no longer worthy to be called your son.' "
— Luke 15:20-21

Commentary

To begin, we need to reiterate that the family and the village are intertwined in first-century village and community life in the Middle East. The father knows how the village feels. There is no doubt that on numerous occasions the villagers told the father that he should never have given his inheritance to his son in the first place. Not only did the father lose, but the village felt they were losers as well. The father knew how the villagers felt and he knew that his son's return to the village would precipitate a crisis and cause a crowd to gather. He was concerned that when his son was identified, he would face verbal and physical abuse. When the father is aware that his son is returning home, he responds immediately. He takes dramatic actions that are calculated to protect his son from the hostility of the villagers.

As soon as the son arrives at the edge of the village, the father runs to meet him. Bailey points out that oriental noblemen with flowing robes would never run (p. 181). Running was shameful because it allowed the ankles to show. It was considered indecent exposure. It indicated a lack of self-control. Jeremias states that it is a most unusual and undignified procedure for an aged oriental father. A son would run to his father, but never would a father run to his son (p. 102). But, the father ran because the need was so

73

urgent. He needed to put himself between his son and the village crowd so as to protect his son. The father is willing to assume a humiliating posture in order to protect him.

The father embraced his son, protecting him from the hostility of the crowd, and kissed him. Shillington points out that "running, embracing, and a kiss are not only the signs of welcome but protection" (p. 156). The son was utterly amazed at his father's action. It was so unexpected, the son was witnessing a visible demonstration of love in humiliation. There were no words appropriate for this moment; the father's acts replace speech. Of this occasion Sa'id writes:

> Christ reports for us the words of the son to his father, but does not give anything about a speech of the father to his son. For in reality the father substitutes kisses for words and replaces assertions with expression and eyes speak for the tongue.— as cited by Bailey, p. 182

The father kissed his son to express his forgiveness. The father hoped that his public display of forgiveness of his son would be the beginning of his son's reconciliation with the village. The father's welcome, embrace, and kiss are clearly an outpouring of grace. Bernard Scott (*Hear Then The Parables*) quotes a rabbinic parallel that makes clear the father's intentions.

> A king had a son who had gone astray from his father a journey of a hundred days. His friends said to him, "Return to your father." He said, "I cannot." Then his father sent to say, "Then return as far as you can, and I will come to you the rest of the way." So God says, "Return to me, and I will return to you."   — p. 117

In the dramatic act of the father's acceptance there is no test of the son's sincerity. Scott suggests that this "initial response indicates that he will not follow a legal or paternal role; he will play the nourishing role" (p. 117). In other words, that father's actions will not be those of legality (well within his rights as an offended father) but of love.

At this point in the parable, the major role is played by the compassionate father. Young suggests that the nature and character of God are made vividly clear by the father's welcome, compassion, and forgiveness (*The Parables of Jesus*, p. 151). As seen in the father's actions, God loves his children even when they make the wrong decisions. The comparison between the compassionate father and God are obvious. God allows his children the freedom to choose, and if the wrong choice brings disaster, he is willing to accept them and forgive them when they return home. On two occasions the father came out and down from the house to face the humiliation and disgrace created by the actions of his lost sons. Regardless of the humiliation and cost, the father came in love and compassion to bring his wayward sons home. This is comparable to the words of the Apostle Paul, "God was in Christ bringing the world back to himself."

In telling this story, Jesus' theme is not only a wayward, lost son, but a father's love. Jeremias declares that this is "a parable of a loving father" (p. 101). For this reason C. H. Dodd places this parable in his grouping of parables under the "parables of the grace of the kingdom" (*Interpreting the Parables*, p. 21). Fitzmyer concludes that the theme of "a loving father" is a symbol of a loving God whom Jesus calls *"Abba Father"* (*Anchor Bible, Luke*, vol. XXXIV, p. 1089). The very first words that a Jewish child learns to speak are *abba* (meaning father) and *imma* (meaning mother). The word *abba* is so personal that no one ever used it to address God until Jesus did. There is not a single example of the use of *abba* as an address of God in the whole of Jewish literature (Fitzmyer, *ibid.*). Jesus' utter intimacy with God is startling. Jesus used this understanding of God that had come to him as a loving and caring Father and placed it in a very earthy, human story so all who heard it would be able to understand how God as Father loves even a lost, confused, and wayward son.

Reflections

The journey back is always a painful and difficult journey. The prodigal's mind was now made up. The period of indecision was now over. He knew what he had to do to overcome the sickness of his soul. The phrase, "So he set off and went to his father," controls all that is to follow. Three steps are involved in his return. First, he comes to himself. He faces the reality of his situation and is honest with himself. This phrase affirms the human capacity to renounce foolish error and reclaim one's heritage and potential. Second, he arises. The journey back begins with the first step. Many times that first step is the most difficult and critical to take, because it reflects a break with the past. It is bringing to an end life as usual. For the prodigal, this first step was an affirmation that his life was taking a different direction. Repentance is followed by action — for the prodigal this action meant putting his trust in his father and returning to his father's house. He now acts on his resolve. Third, he goes to his father. This is the most critical step, because he is casting himself on his father's mercy.

The focus is now on the father. It is quite possible that after all of this time the father has assumed that his son has failed and that he is possibly dead. The son had no idea how much his father had missed him and how his father's heart burned with immense desire to bring his child home. The son had no idea the number of times the father would look up from his chores, lean on his hoe, and gaze down a distant path to see if his son was coming home. Each time he would think to himself, "He'll come. If not today then another day." Numerous times he would wake up in the middle of the night certain that he had heard his son's voice cry out, "Father! Father!" Hurrying to his room he would throw open the door only to discover an empty bed, just as it had been since the day he left. Each day he continued to place the son's plate and utensils at the dinner table — just in case.

Then it happened. "While he was still far off, his father saw him and was filled with compassion." Notice that "his father saw him." His father saw his wretched condition. He saw his helplessness. He saw his broken spirit. He saw his despair. He saw his lowered head and slumped shoulders. He saw his tattered and filthy clothes. But he saw something more — he saw his son. From a distance the father saw his pain and shame. He saw what the distant land had done to his son. The father does not inquire as to the reason for his son's return. He does not scold, "What are you doing here? When you run out of money you return home. Are you sorry for all the pain and heartache you brought to me? Do you expect me to let you in after all you have done? Get your life straightened out before you expect me to take you back." Nothing like that ever happened. Instead, we have the three greatest words in this entire narrative: "filled with compassion." That is the one thing a father or mother will never relinquish in regard to their son or daughter — is compassion. Parents may not understand or fathom certain behavior or lifestyle, but they will always have compassion. As parents we know that God's love for us is so real and intense, and that God would search for us to the ends of the earth. How could we do anything less for our children?

Immediately upon recognizing him, the father runs toward his son. It would have been humiliating for an Oriental nobleman with flowing robes to run anywhere. In Eastern eyes it was undignified for an elderly man to run. Not only was it shameful (baring his ankles) for an elderly man to run, it also indicated a lack of self-control. But the father has good reason to run. This is an emergency and his son is in trouble. As his son enters the village, the father knows the villagers will gather around. The son will be the subject of taunts and perhaps verbal and physical abuse. Under such circumstances surely a father would run. Shillington points out that the Greek term used here, *dramon*, means to exert oneself to the limit of one's powers. Obviously, the father acts this way because he believes his son is in serious trouble. He runs with compassion because he is concerned for his son and he wants to protect him from the humiliating experience of facing the home-town crowd. He runs with compassion to put himself between his son and the hostile, jeering crowd. He wants to get there before they do. The event draws a crowd. The villagers come because they want to voice their protest to the son and they want to see what the returning son looks like and how his father will respond. In an act of humility and acceptance, the father hugs his son, embraces him, and kisses him. In mid-eastern culture the kiss was a sign of public reconciliation. The father's action was not only to reconcile his son to the family, but also to reconcile himself and his family to the village.

The son is so overwhelmed by his father's love and acceptance that he delivers only part of his prepared speech, "Father, I have sinned against heaven and before you; I am no longer worthy to be called your son." The part about the "hired servant" is missing. He is embarrassed to speak such words of his own scheming plan of reconciliation in the face of the father's outpouring of love and grace. In seeing his father's eyes filled with tears, he notices that his father is different from when he left. His face is hollow, drawn, and lined. His shoulders stooped, he appears so much older and worn than when he left. The son says to himself, "O God, what have I done to my father?" He now realizes that his sin was not the lost money, but his broken relationship with his father. He understands that any new relationship must be the pure gift of the father's love. He offered no solution; that is why he refrained from speaking the latter part of his prepared speech. To assume that he could compensate his father with his labor was now an insult. "I am no longer worthy to be your son" is the only appropriate response.

The father makes his reconciliation public. The son now enters the village under the protective loving care of his father. Both the son and the crowd that gathered are astonished at what they are seeing. Rather than experiencing ruthless hostility that was expected by all parties, instead they witness an unexpected, visible demonstration of love and humility on the part of the father. The father's actions replace speech. There are no words of acceptance and welcome. The love expressed is too profound for words. Nouwen reminds us that never has God's immense, compassionate love been expressed in such a poignant way as it is here in these verses of Luke 15. He points out that everything comes together. "Time and eternity intersect. Approaching death and everlasting life touch each other. Sin and forgiveness embrace. The human and the divine become one" (*The Return of the Prodigal*, p. 88). Things are so different now in the journey back. He is coming home in his shame and helplessness. In leaving, his demand was, "Give me!" His words were, "My inheritance. My portion.

My freedom." He left with demands, but he returns with confession: "I have sinned. Forgive me. Restore me. Will you take me back?" In leaving, he thought that freedom was to be found away from his father. Freedom was now with the father. He was to discover that the more dependent he was on his father, the freer he would become.

Now that he is in the loving embrace of his father — what did he learn in a distant land? He learned a great deal about his illusions, miscalculations, poor judgments, and limitations, and a great deal about the meaning of freedom. Above all he learned about his father's love. He discovered the breadth and depth of that love. Look what he had to go through in order to learn all of this. He paid a high price for all of his newly acquired knowledge. When one pays such a high price for such knowledge, it is important to get everything that the experience has to teach. Some people pay an enormously high price for some of the most basic and elementary lessons of life. Some experience bankruptcy in money and spirit; some go through long periods of separation from family and friends. For others things may be more drastic, such as a prison sentence, or a lifetime in AA, or a painful period in mental and spiritual rehabilitation. The tragedy is that a person may go through such an experience, paying an enormously high price, and still never learn anything from it.

Interestingly, the writer Henri Nouwen and the biblical scholar Kenneth E. Bailey both see the father's actions as that of a mother. They arrive at their conclusions from different directions — Nouwen from his visit to the Hermitage in St. Petersburg, Russia, where he was captivated by Rembrandt's *The Prodigal Son*; Bailey from his cultural-historical approach to the study of the text. For Nouwen it was the father's hands in the Rembrandt painting that captured his attention. The father's hands were the center of the painting for him. As he studied the hands, he noticed that they were quite different. He noticed that the left hand as it was touching the son's shoulder is strong and masculine. The fingers are spread out and they cover a large part of the prodigal's shoulders and back. Not only do they seem to touch, but they appear to hold and embrace. The left hand reveals the firm grip of a father's strong, masculine hand.

The right hand is different. It is narrower than the left hand and does not hold and grip as the left does. The right hand appears re-fined, soft, very tender, with long and slender fingers which appear eloquent and close together. The left hand seems to extend a firm grip; the right hand lies gently on the son's shoulders. The right hand seeks to caress, stroke, and offer consolation and comfort. After long hours of studying Rembrandt's masterpiece, Nouwen concluded that the left hand is a father's hand, whereas the right hand is a mother's hand. As he looked at Rembrandt's old man bending over his returning son touching his shoulder with his hands, he said, "I see not only a father who clasps his son in his arms. But also a mother who caresses her child, surrounds him with the warmth of her body and holds him against the womb from which he sprang." For Nouwen, the "return of the prodigal becomes the return to God's womb, the return to the very origins of being and echoes again Jesus' exhortation to Nicodemus, 'Truly I say to you unless you be born anew, you cannot see the kingdom of God' " (*The Return of the Prodigal*, p. 94).

Bailey points out that a traditional oriental patriarch would be expected to sit in isolation in his house and wait for his wayward son to come to him and give him an account of his actions. He would never run out to him. It would be the mother who would run down the road, hug her son, and kiss him. Bailey suggests:

> *A 1,000-year-old, finely tuned sacred tradition is avail-able to Jesus. The prophets called God "Father" and partially described that father in female terms. This language affirmed the personhood and unity of God for all believers, male and female. In the Old Testa-ment, God is already presented as a father who also acts with the tender compassion of a mother (Deuter-onomy 32:18; Psalm 131; Isaiah 42:14, 66:13). The Dead Sea Scrolls describe God with the same imagery ... in 1 John, the believer is "born of God." That is, God "gives birth" in the New Testament even as God does in the Old (Deuteronomy 32:18). In this parable,*

too, the father appears on the road, demonstrating the
tender compassion of a mother.
— *Christianity Today*, October 26, 1998, p. 34

I am aware that the scriptures speak to us of God in many voices, but never more persuasively than when it sounds and sends forth the maternal note of God's love. For centuries Christian people have overlooked the Bible's use of motherhood as a metaphor for God. There is an historical reason for this. The biblical metaphors for God as father, king, and lord were used in a time when monarchy was the seat of political power. God's sovereignty was expressed in terms of royalty and kingship. In an agricultural economy, it was inevitable that the poetic imagery for God's tender concern and care should be drawn from a shepherd and his flock. In a patriarchal society, where the father figure was dominant, thoughts of God's relationship to his people would center around the idea of the father. These metaphors and images functioned well for those days, but the world has changed. Today, the use of the word "father" as a metaphor for God is not a very suitable symbol for many of the world's children. As Bailey has pointed out, although the biblical writers made strong use of masculine imagery and metaphors, there are signs in both the Old and New Testaments that the motherhood of God was on their minds. In the Old Testament this loving God is the Mother who has given us the birth of creation that we know and see, and in the New Testament it is the one through whom the miracle of rebirth takes place and brings us the joy of Christian living.

Marguerite Henry Atkins wrote a remarkable book telling about the years of caring for her husband who had Alzheimer's disease. *Also My Journey* is a vivid account of her struggle, pain, anguish, and the hope of faith. She wrote this poem just before her husband's death.

He is my loved one,
But thou didst create him
and so lovest him more.
I know that thou wilt be near him
In his death ...

Thou wilt hold him close in thy arms
as a mother cradles her child
while sleeping.

That image of God as mother brought her hope and comfort. She could visualize how in death God was near to her husband, holding him close, as a mother who cradles her child. In the same way Nouwen declares, "I see not only a father who clasps his son's arms. But also a mother who caresses her child, surrounds him with the warmth of her body, and holds him against the womb from which he sprang" (p. 94).

It is evident that with verse 20, the view shifts from the returning son to the waiting father. As Jesus describes the prodigal's father in terms of goodness, grace, and abounding love, his main purpose is to reveal the nature and character of God. This is the kind of God I want to believe in: a God who from the beginning of creation has stretched out his arms saying, "Let there be light and life!"; who continues to stretch out his arms saying, "Come unto me all who labor and are heavy laden." God's arms are outstretched and they are ever waiting. God is never letting his arms drop in despair. God is ever waiting to let his longing arms embrace a returning son or daughter. God's only desire is to welcome back, to bless, and to embrace. As he told this part of the parable, I can imagine how Jesus must have used his hands and his arms — opening his palms and stretching out his arms as wide as possible, suggesting, "Yes! Yes! You can come home!" The nails of the cross continue to hold open the arms of Christ for every wayward, bewildered son or daughter who happens to be lost and alone in a distant land — as well as the prodigal that stays home.

David Watson states, "Jesus is the missing person in his own parable" (*God Does Not Foreclose*, p. 94). In him we have the assurance that God wants all people to be part of his heavenly family. When we look at the cross, we realize how much God was willing to risk, and continues to risk, to have all prodigals back home. God's extended invitation from the cross makes clear how serious the human condition is and how intense and far-reaching God's love is for all who stray from the Father's house. It is through the love and grace that are so clearly seen in the parable that all who are reconciled to God are in a new relationship that can best be described in two words: *Welcome home!* The purpose of Jesus' ministry is to make this homecoming possible for everyone. Watson concludes, "Jesus gives this parable new meaning by being the person to invite us back home and by giving his life to bring all prodigals to their senses" (p. 95).

The story is told about a venerable old sage who asked his disciples the question, "How can you know when the darkness is leaving and the dawn is coming?" "When we can see a tree in the distance and know that it is an elm and not a juniper," ventured one student. "When we can see an animal and know that it is a fox and not a wolf," chimed in another. "No," said the old man, "those things will not help us." Puzzled, the students demanded, "How then can we know?" The master teacher drew himself up to his full stature and replied quietly, "We know the darkness is leaving and the dawn is coming when we can see another person's face and know that this is our brother and sister; otherwise, no matter what time it is, it is still dark." The prodigal knew that it was the dawning of a new day when he saw the tears streaming down his father's face, a face hollow and worn by the pain of waiting for a wayward, lost son to return. Now, let the celebration begin.

Discussion Questions

1. **Humiliation.** In what way did the father face a humiliating situation in his son's return to the village? How many times in the parable did the father face humiliation? If the father represents God in the parable, what does the father's action regarding his son's return tell you about God?

2. **Love.** Jeremias declares that this is really "a parable of a loving father." Do you agree that the theme is not that of a wayward, lost son, but of a father's love? What about the thought that Jesus uses this human story so all who hear it would be able to understand that God loves even a lost, confused, and

wayward son and welcomes him home? Is this the kind of God you know?

3. **Compassion.** The key phrase in the parable is "filled with compassion." Do you agree that the one thing a father and mother will never relinquish in regard to a rebellious son or daughter is compassion, regardless of how far they have wandered? What has been your experience as a parent or as a child?

4. **Reconciliation.** The father is speechless when he first meets his son. There is a kiss and a hug, something a father would never do in public. Could it be that the love expressed is too profound for words? Do you agree with the conclusion that never has God's immense, compassionate love been expressed in such a poignant way as it is in this parable?

5. **Knowledge.** The prodigal paid a very high price for his newly acquired knowledge. When one pays such a high price for such knowledge, it is important to get everything that experience has to teach. What price have you paid for the knowledge you obtained regarding yourself and God?

6. **Metaphors.** Several scholars have seen the motherhood and fatherhood of God in the son's return. Why is it that the biblical metaphors for the motherhood of God are overlooked? What are the cultural reasons for this? What is your response?

Prayer
Lord, I hear your voice calling me through so many different voices, happenings, events, and people. But what you are saying seems too good to be true — beyond belief. You have said if I confess, you will forgive; if I knock, you will open; if I come to you weary and heavyhearted, you will give me comfort and rest.

Lord, I believe, but help my unbelief. Help me to get over the barriers and the obstacles that keep me from coming to you. Help me to take that first step so I can begin my journey home. Amen.

Chapter Six

Celebration

"But the father said to his slaves, 'Quickly, bring out a robe — the best one — and put it on him; put a ring on his finger and sandals on his feet. And get the fatted calf and kill it, and let us eat and celebrate; for this son of mine was dead and is alive again; he was lost and is found!' And they began to celebrate."   — Luke 15:22-24

Commentary

Although the son had an elaborate speech prepared, the father never gave him a chance to finish it. Scholars assert that the prodigal is coming home with a rabbinic understanding of repentance. His prepared speech is shattered by his father's demonstration of love in humiliation. Because he was coming home in a state of apprehension and fear, the love and acceptance that he received were emotionally overwhelming. He now realizes that he cannot offer a solution to their ongoing relationship and that the point is not the lost money, but rather the broken relationship and that any new relationship must be a pure gift from his father. In fact, at this point he can offer no solution. For him to assume that he can compensate his father with his labor and work is an insult. His only response is, "I am unworthy...." The Arabic scholar Ibin al-pTayyib says that the son changed his mind not to present his prepared speech because "of what he saw in his father's love" (quoted by Bailey, p. 184). Because his father's love was so demonstrative and visible, the son now felt compelled to change his procedure. This change resulted in his repentance, "Father, I have sinned ... I am no longer worthy to be called your son."

After the son's confession and repentance, the father addresses the servants. It appears that the servants are there at the entrance of the village with the rest of the crowd, eagerly waiting for some clue from the father as to how they should treat the son. "If the father had indicated displeasure with so much as an indifferent shrug of the shoulder, the servants would have done nothing for him" (Bailey, p. 185). The father commands the servants, "Quickly, bring out a robe — the best one — and put it on him; put a ring on his finger and sandals on his feet" (v. 22). The robe was probably the one that the father wore on feast days and other important occasions. When the guests arrived at the feast and saw the father's best robe draped over his son's shoulders, the father knew it assured the complete acceptance of the son's reconciliation by the entire community. The ceremonial robe in the East is a mark of high distinction. The investiture with such a robe of distinction is evidence of a new relationship.

Jeremias believes that the robe has eschatological significance. Isaiah 61:10 is given special attention in the teachings of Jesus, "For he clothed me with the garments of salvation, he has covered me with the robe of righteousness" (*The Parables of Jesus*, p. 102f). It may be remembered that Jesus spoke of the Messianic Age as a new garment (Mark 2:21), and that he compared forgiveness with the best robe with which the father clothed the prodigal (Luke 15:22); hence we cannot doubt that it is this comparison that underlies Matthew 22:11-13. The father admonishes his servants to get the best robe and "put it on him." In essence the father is saying, "All of the marks of a far country must be covered." It has been pointed out that this investiture with the new garment is therefore the symbol of the New Age (Jeremias, *ibid.*). Thus, what could have been a confrontation became a coronation. What made the difference — the son's confession and the father's love.

Excavations reveal that the ring is to be regarded as a signet ring (Scott, *Hear Then The Parables*, p. 118). The signet ring enabled the son once more to make documents with his own sign, thus implicitly giving him authority in the household. Not only through the ring has the father bestowed authority, but also by confidence, in that he trusts his son to handle his newly restored authority wisely.

A servant was barefoot, having no shoes. The father commands the servants to put shoes on the son's feet indicating that he was a free man who would no longer go barefoot as a servant. The servants placing sandals on the son's feet was a sign that they accepted him as their master — no order could have expressed this more conclusively. The father's command also indicates that he intends to ignore his son's request "make me one of your hired servants." The son's place, which has been abrogated by his loss of property, is now restored.

Lastly the father orders that the fatted calf be killed and the party should begin. The killing of the fatted calf and the feast are related to the fact that the son has been starving and now he will be fed. Bailey suggests that the selection of a calf rather than a sheep or goat means that the entire village is invited (p. 186). Only rarely did they eat meat at all (Jeremias, p. 103), and because of the short time in which the meat would spoil, they would not prepare a quantity that would not be consumed. Now, in honor of the son, the calf would be prepared, and it was sufficient food for the entire village to take part in the celebration.

In the first century in the Middle East, a feast was a gesture of solidarity and respect for those involved. The purpose of such a banquet includes a desire to reconcile the son to the whole community. That is exactly what the father expected this feast to be: a reconciliation of son to family and of son and family to the village. But the father was taking a huge risk: What if nobody came? If the villagers did not come, it would indicate how displeased and offended they were by the son's behavior. If that happened, the family would be worse off than they were before. As the listeners heard the narrative unfold, the drama was heightened for them when the father made the first move toward the village and risked disastrous rejection. The hearers naturally wondered what the outcome would be, and they would have been on edge until they learned that the villagers showed up and reconciliation was achieved.

The joy that was known by the shepherd in the earlier parable of Luke 15 and that came to the woman in her discovery of the lost coin is now the same joy that is experienced by the father in the return of his lost son. The joy of celebration also encompassed the hearers. The hearers rejoiced with the father in the return of his son, identifying with the father's joy and the son's obvious relief.

I told this story to a group of youth who listened attentively as though they had never heard it before. When I got to the part where the father saw his son coming down the path toward home, I said to them, "What do you think the father did?" And one boy blurted out, "He killed him!" When the youth laughed at his response, he said, "If I did that to my father, he would kill me!" I believe that some of the listeners to this story would probably have had the same reaction, and they were amazed at the father's love and acceptance.

Robert Capon in his inimitable style suggests that the fatted calf is actually the Christ-figure in the parable. He asks, "What does the fatted calf do?" It stands around in its stall for one purpose in life, to drop dead at a moment's notice in order that people may have a party. "If that doesn't sound like the lamb slain from the foundation of the earth ... I don't know what does. The fatted calf proclaims that the party is what the father's house is all about, just as Jesus, the dead and risen Bridegroom, proclaims that an eternal bash is what the universe is all about. Creation is not ultimately about religion, or spirituality, or morality, or reconciliation, or any other solemn subject; it's about God having a good time and just itching to share it" (*The Parables of Grace*, p. 141).

Bailey points out that the story now has come full circle. He states that the literary structure can now be more fully understood. And that in light of the underlying culture it is of particular interest to compare the son's first speech at the beginning and his second speech in the center. He states that each line has its match and this can be seen as follows:

Speech 1
a. Father
b. give me my share of property
c. he divided his living.

Speech II
a. Father
b. I have sinned against heaven and you
c. I am no more worthy to be called your son. (p. 187)

Thus the literary structure reinforces the cultural elements in determining the movement of the story.

The homecoming scene presents the picture of a servant who plans to confess and compensate. The father then demonstrates unexpected love in humiliation. The would-be-servant is overwhelmed by grace and becomes a son. Bailey declares that the scene provides a new understanding of repentance as acceptance of grace and the confession of unworthiness. The two rejoice together. At the end of the father's speech, the son still has the option of preferring the freedom of an independent status in the village, far from the complications of living with his older brother. But the son accepts the father's grace — grace wins! Now the son and the father can begin to make merry. Indeed the lost is found.

Scholars have raised the question: Are there any christological implications of the homecoming scene? The apparent absence of any reference in the parable to the work of Christ has been a problem that scholars have sought to answer in recent times. Of all of the answers that have been set forth in recent scholarship, there is one that seems to have more significance than any of the others, that being: after all the parable is not a "complete compendium of theology" and we should not treat it as such. Those advocating this approach state, "The parable teaches that God loves sinners *while* they are still sinners. That is enough. We should not expect a full theological statement. To make this a complete compendium of theology would utterly destroy the parable as we know it" (Bailey, p. 188). At the same time, the parable does reveal how women and men are reconciled to God. This parable is extraordinary in composition. It states God's fundamental principle of grace in dealing with sinners in an unforgettable manner. Anything that would diminish this principle or alter its composition or clarity in order to gain greater theological insight would be unthinkable.

In answering the question regarding the christological implications of the homecoming scene, Charles Gublin, in his *Theological Considerations on Luke 15* (p. 30), provides one of the most stimulating responses. He does not violate the cultural influences that inform the text nor does he introduce some new type of allegorizing. He points out that Christ's redemptive love is reflected in the activity of his public life, not just on Calvary. In the subtle portrayal of redemptive love in Luke 15, Jesus is the one in and through whom the heavenly joy is shown to women and men. Thus, the Father is seen in and through Jesus' contact with women and men. Jesus himself is the efficacious sign of the reconciliation and new life.

Interestingly, Bailey expands Gublin's comments with significant insight. He suggests that for the Palestinian listeners the father in the parable would be a natural symbol for God. He quotes Isaiah 63:16, "For you are our father...." As the parable progresses, the father comes out of the house and in a very dramatic way demonstrates unexpected love publicly in humiliation. Surely Jesus intended his listeners to see in this act a dramatic example of how he welcomes sinners. Bailey concludes that when the father leaves the house to come out to his son in love and humility, he demonstrates at least a part of the meaning of the incarnation and the atonement (Bailey, p. 190). Jeremias is right when he states, "The parable should be called the parable of the father's love." Obviously the parable is taken from a life situation, thus the father is not God, but an earthly father, yet some of the expressions used are meant that in his love he is an image of God (p. 101).

What if the father would not have come out from the house and made such a public display of his love in such humility? He would have had merely another servant. But, if the father goes out and in a shattering and humiliating demonstration expresses that love, then the son will see it and hopefully understand it. If this happens, then the father will have a son. In conclusion, then, the atonement is at least "overheard" in the parable.

Reflections

This remarkable parable describes with the most impressive simplicity what God is like. With clarity it expresses God's goodness, grace, great mercy, and abounding love. God rejoices over the return of the lost, like a father who prepared a feast of welcome. The very heart of the New Testament message of *good news* is that God wants a homecoming for everyone!

What does the parable tell us about the nature and character of God? First, that God comes to us where we are. This has always been most difficult for us to comprehend, yet the parable drives this point home with the utmost clarity. In order for the homecoming to take place, the father *came out from his house and down the road* to the entrance of the village to welcome his estranged son back home. This has the impact of the incarnation, of God becoming flesh and dwelling among us — God coming to us where we are. Just as the son was so astonished by seeing his father at the entrance of village welcoming him home, we also are astonished by the fact that God could be so down-to-earth, that God would come to us on such human and ordinary terms. But when one reflects on the biblical narrative, it becomes evident that God shuns the spectacular and uses the ordinary. What is more casual or ordinary than the birth of a child? The babe in Bethlehem always appears to be less than he really is: like a child born in obscurity; like a young man growing up and being unnoticed for years while living in a carpenter shop in Nazareth; like a prisoner refusing to answer the false accusations of a judge; and, like an ordinary man riding on the back of a donkey. How odd of God to be so casual and so down-to-earth. In a surprising move that startles the town folk as well as the gaunt, careworn son, the father runs to the entrance of the village to welcome his son home.

Second, the parable helps us to comprehend that the good news of the gospel is that Christ meets us at the level of our need. Think of this good news in regard to the person who is living on $100 a year. He has no car. His home is the size of a backyard tool shed. He has no television, radio, or appliances, and is without the benefit of running water or electricity. He represents over half of the world's population. For such people, the words of Jesus are good news indeed.

On September 11, 2001, a tremendous horror was unleashed upon our land, unthinkable as to its destruction of both property and human life. We were stunned. It could not happen to us. Not in the United States. Not only did the clouds of destruction engulf New York City, but the clouds of despair engulfed our hearts and lives. Our optimism and self-assurance were shaken to the core. We were told by many that things will never be the same again. We who were not near the World Trade Center have no idea of the carnage, pain, and intense suffering. The world at one moment was so stable, secure, fixed, and reliable, but in an instant it appeared so fragile. William Willimon, chaplain at the Duke University Chapel, said as he entered the pulpit on the Sunday after September 11, that he never had sensed in all of his ministry people so hungry for the Word. He said most of the time we preachers are ignored, but not that week. He had calls from reporters at BBC, CNN, and local newspapers all asking him the same question, "What are you going to preach on Sunday?" The world wanted to hear a good sermon in the worst way. He left the lectionary that Sunday and chose the text from Genesis 1:1-5, *Then God said, "Let there be light"; and there was light. And God saw that the light was good.*

The good news of Luke 15 is still the good news today — that God comes to us at the level of our need. In the face of the horror of September 11, many asked, "Where is God?" God is right where God has always been, seeking, loving, comforting, guiding, caring for all his children. On September 16, 2001, when Peter Gomes was preaching at Memorial Church at Harvard, students wanted to know, "Where is God?" Gomes answered, "God is to be found where God is most needed — in trouble, sorrow, sickness, adversity, and even death itself. God is where God is always, by the side of those who need God the most" (Willimon, *The Sunday After Tuesday: College Pupits Respond to 9-11*, p. 95). In the last several months many have experienced tragedy, suffering, and loss as never before, but at the same time many have experienced the sustaining presence of God's love and grace as never before. The words from Isaiah burst upon the scene with new meaning and significance for many:

> *Comfort, O comfort my people, says your God ... He gives power to the faint, and strengthens the powerless ... But those who wait for the Lord shall renew their strength....*
> — vv. 1, 29, 31a

The prodigal's father came out to the village gate to welcome his son home. He met his son at the level of his shame and despair. Today, God comes to us in Christ and meets us at the level of our despair, our heavy-heartedness, and our abandonment and asks, "Where does it hurt and how can I help?"

Such a discovery of grace and hope leads to celebration. When Jesus describes God's kingdom as a joyful banquet, celebration is often at the center. This is what happens in the parable: the father is overcome with joy, the joy of a lost son's return and redemption. The father throws an elaborate party and everybody is invited to the celebration. In the New Testament context an invitation to a meal is an invitation to intimacy with God. Nouwen points out that this is especially clear at the time of the Last Supper (pp. 10-16). Jesus says to his disciples, "From now on I tell you, I shall never again drink wine until the day I drink the new wine with you in the kingdom of my father" (Matthew 26:29). The liturgy of Holy Communion picks up the same theme when it states, "Until Christ comes in final victory and we feast at his heavenly banquet." Again at the end of the New Testament God's ultimate victory is described as a splendid wedding feast, "... blessed are those who are invited to the wedding feast of the lamb."

Celebration belongs to the kingdom of God, because all within the kingdom have experienced forgiveness, reconciliation, healing, and, above all, transformation. We will rejoice in the kingdom because we all have been lost and found; we all were dead and are alive again. Celebration is the hallmark of Luke 15. It is the theme that runs through every one of its parables. "*Rejoice with me*," the shepherd says, "I have found my lost sheep." "*Rejoice with me*," says the woman, "I have found my lost coin."

"*Rejoice with me*," says the father, "this son of mine was lost and is now found."

Nouwen reminds us that all of these voices are the voice of God. God does not want to keep his joy to himself. He wants everyone to share in it. God's joy is the joy of his angels and his saints. It is the joy of all who belong to the Kingdom. The very heart of the New Testament message of good news is that God wants a homecoming for everyone. Capon states, "If we were to sum up the parable to this point thus far, it would be nothing but hilariously good news; the father, the prodigal, and the fatted calf are all dead; they are all three risen (the calf, admittedly, as a veal roast — but then, you can't have everything); and everybody is having a ball. As Jesus put it succinctly, 'They began to be merry' " (p. 142).

We are all invited to celebrate the joy of the Lord. This is the very reason that Jesus told this parable so all could enter into this joy. Nouwen reminds us, "From God's perspective, one hidden act of repentance, one little gesture of selfless love, one moment of true forgiveness is all that is needed to bring God from his throne to run to his returning son and to fill the heavens with sounds of divine joy" (*The Parables of Grace*, p. 108). The remarkable thing is that God's joy can be our joy as well. Come to the party!

Discussion Questions

1. **Unworthy.** The prodigal had a prayer and a proposition to offer his father. He was so overwhelmed by his father's love and acceptance, they now appeared as being out of place. His response was, "I am unworthy...." Have you experienced such a feeling of unworthiness in God's presence? Explain.

2. **Acceptance.** At the father's command, the servants are asked to provide certain items for the son. What is the significance of the robe? Ring? Sandals? Fatted calf? Do you think the father's public demonstration of his love for his son was done to assure the son's acceptance by the community?

3. **Risk.** The father took an enormous public risk. His son could reject his love and the community could reject his offer to come to the feast to welcome his son back home. Thinking of the father as representing God, what risk has God taken in this world? What risk has God taken with you? How does the parable help you understand your relationship with God?

4. **Celebration.** It is only natural that such a discovery of grace and hope would lead to celebration, so the father throws a party. Celebration is the hallmark of Luke 15. All three parables, regarding the shepherd, the woman, and the father, contain the same phrase — "Rejoice with me." How does the church, the body of Christ, celebrate such hope and grace? How do you personally celebrate it?

5. **Joy.** Jesus told this parable to explain to the religious leaders, who were so critical of him, why there was joy in heaven over one sinner who repents. Do you believe God wants a joyful homecoming for everybody? How would people know you are a joyful person?

Prayer

Forgive me, Lord, for not being honest with you. How many times have I come to you with my own agenda, plans, preconceived prayers, wanting to make a deal, only to go away in disappointment and despair? Help me to understand how much you love and accept me for what and who I am. Warts and all.

How much, O Lord, I desire to be part of the celebration and I am longing for someone to say to me, "You were lost but now you are found." Lord, I so much want to put on a funny hat and come to the party where I can celebrate a new life, a new hope, and a new beginning. Amen.

Chapter Seven

A Stranger In One's Own House

"... 'Listen! For all of these years I have been working as a slave for you, and I have never disobeyed your command; yet you have never given me even a young goat so that I might celebrate with my friends. But when this son of yours came back, who has devoured your property with prostitutes, you killed the fatted calf for him!' Then the father said to him, 'Son, you are always with me, and all that is mine is yours. But we had to celebrate and rejoice, because this brother of yours was dead and has come to life; he was lost and has been found.' "

— Luke 15:29-32

Commentary

Scholars have pointed out that this is basically one parable with two parts and the second half of the parable (15:25-32) is culturally and stylistically a repetition of the first half. The externals are different but the essential nature of each is the same. Furthermore, the father's response to each of his sons is essentially identical.

Why did Jesus include it? For Jeremias there is only one answer, because of the setting in which the parable took place. "The parable was addressed to men who were like the elder brother, men who were offended by the gospel. It was an appeal to their conscience. Jesus' hearers were in the position of the elder son who had to decide whether they would accept his father's invitation and share his joy" (*The Parables of Jesus*, p. 104). As Jesus told this parable he was well aware of his critics who were listening to him. They were critical not only of his message but of his social activities as well. Therefore in this second part of the parable he was justifying his socializing and eating with sinners and outcasts. He was hopeful that they would abandon their self-righteous criticism and experience the joy that the good news brings.

In the latter part of the parable the father takes a more prominent role in the dialogue and interaction with the elder son. Young points out that the two sons are quite similar. Both view their father more as a banker than a father. The father is the master who controls the finances and they are the laborers who desire more money. Both sons speak of their relationship with their father from their financial ties and work obligations. They view themselves as hired servants in their father's house. "As heirs, the younger son wants unlimited overdraft — the elder son desires a fat savings account with the prestige of wealth and position. While they seem so different in the way they go about obtaining what they want, they are really quite similar" (p. 156). The actions of both sons produce the same results — a broken relationship with the father. The young son is alienated from his father by rebellion, passion, and greed. The elder son is alienated from his father by hatred and resentment.

It appears that the elder son is attacking his brother with definite intent in mind. If he can demonstrate that his younger brother is a rebellious son, then, according to the law in Deuteronomy 21:18-21, he can be put to death. The elder son paints a very black picture indeed regarding his younger brother, because he brings up the charge of prostitutes. This is the first time that any sexual immorality regarding the younger son has been raised against him. One gets the feeling at this point that the elder son is reaching for straws. He was reminding his father that the money his son had spent on prostitutes was money that was to take care of his father in his old age. He is saying to his father, "This son of yours really doesn't care for you. If he did, he would have used his money in a different manner, by showing you respect."

The interaction between the father and the elder son is remarkable. The dialogue between them reveals the father's love and compassion for his resentful son. Where the son sees himself as a faithful slave, the father views him as a companion: "Son, you are always with me." The father considers him as co-owner of the farm,

"All that is mine is yours." The son had no need to earn his father's approval, he already had it.

Reflections

The young son bolts defiantly from his father and family and goes off in a huff to a distant land. He blows his entire inheritance on loose living and comes back home in disgrace. The father gets carried away and throws a party for everybody in the whole community. What a great place to stop the story. But Jesus did not stop there. The truth is, he could not omit the latter part of the story because that is the part that deals with most of us. Most of us did not travel to a distant land, we just stayed at home and pouted. Not all prodigals leave; some remain and become strangers in their own house.

Through the years the older brother's behavior appeared as being right, proper, sober, and respectable. The town's people thought of him as "the good boy who stayed at home and cared for his aging father." It was the younger son who had all the problems, made self-evident by his sins of passion. The older brother's sins of disposition and attitude were less obvious — but potentially more destructive to the family. There was a time when the character of church members was judged by what they did not do. They did not gamble, play cards, dance, go to the theatre, or drink. But many of the those good church members who also served as stewards and deacons were slave owners, slum lords, employers of child labor, and abusive to their wives and children. The fact is there are those who remain in the father's house and decline inwardly.

The elder son is out in the field. When he hears the music coming from the house, he is suspicious. By the beat of the music, he knows that it is a joyous occasion. Living recently in an African village, I have learned that rhythms are specific and known. The older son does not rush in; he is suspicious that this may have something to do with his brother's return. His fear is that the old man is getting carried away with emotion. When one of his servants told him that his brother had returned and that his father had killed the fatted calf — his suspicions were confirmed. Custom required his presence. In the Hebrew community, at such a celebration and banquet the elder son has special responsibilities. But he is not anxious to assume them. The older son's refusal to come in and be part of the celebration is totally unexpected. It is shocking. Again, the family is the victim of public humiliation and the father has another rebellious son on his hands. It is the public humiliation of the family that captures the attention of any Middle Eastern hearer/reader.

The elder son's behavior now grabs the attention of the hearers because he appears so aggravated by all that has happened. The elder son is resistant to his father's plea that he come to the party. Everything has gone against the elder son's plans for his life. This is not what he anticipated; he had different plans. But his plans are now being jeopardized by the return of his wayward brother. Because of his brother's lost inheritance, he is fearful that as the eldest son he will be responsible for the sole support of his aged father and possibly for his younger brother as well. His planned retirement has collapsed. He has that sinking Enron feeling — that his 401K retirement fund has just disintegrated. His interests have been seriously damaged. He is mad. He is angry. He doesn't care who knows about it. To the father's chagrin, the entire village again has been drawn into the family quarrel. This is the kind of thing that families seek to camouflage and keep from the neighbors.

The question is asked: How could this elder son remain at home, live in the father's house, and become for so many years the recipient of the father's love and goodwill and yet drift so far from his father, to the point that he becomes a stranger? This happened in the same way people can live for a lifetime as members of a Christian church and not have the slightest idea of what takes place there. They have no concept of Christian love or reconciling grace. On the campus of Harvard University, a friend said to Richard Niebuhr, "There goes one of your students." His reply was, "No, he attends my classes, but he is not one of my students." There is a difference. I could imagine someone saying to Jesus, "Lord, there goes one of your disciples." "No," Jesus replies, "he attends one of my churches, but he is not one of my disciples." Is it possible that a person can remain within the church and shrivel and deteriorate inwardly and spiritually? There are those who mis-construe Jesus' comment to remain childlike to mean to become childish — remaining immature in faith and vision. Judas traveled within the company of the twelve, but something went wrong, something never connected, somehow he never caught what was taking place. He was clueless. It all seemed to go right past him.

The elder brother was ticked-off. He was not ticked-off by his brother's return, but rather he was upset because he felt he had gotten a raw deal. He was willing for his brother to come home, but to penance and not to a party. He said to himself, "What moral instruction is there in such action?" He felt that the father was saying to his brother that it's all right to mess around and screw up. The elder brother wanted to say to his father, "What about being responsible for one's actions? Doesn't one reap what one sows? What kind of world would this be if we made a practice of rewarding sons for their rebellious actions while God-fearing folks are still out in the fields hard at work?" Robert Capon has sug-gested that when the elder son hears that the father wants to kill the prized fatted calf he is enraged. He rants, "The fatted calf! Does the old man know that I have been saving that prize calf for next month's sales promotion when we are going to show our new line of turnips? How can I run a business when he blows the entire advertising budget for entertainment on that loser of a son?" (*The Parables of Grace*, p. 142). To say the least, he was angry and he was not about to go into the party.

Many identify with the elder son. The son's anger and resent-ment shut him out from the party and the rest of the family. Many have felt this rage. Feeling left out and excluded creates a desire to be alone and in our isolation we cut ourselves off from those whom we so desperately need. The elder son needs to be with the rest of his family. However, he reflects on the state of affairs and quickly decides not to enter the house. In this cultural setting, an elder son has specific responsibilities at such an official banquet. He is sup-posed to move among the guests, making certain they are com-fortable, getting enough to eat and seeing to it that the servants are carrying out their tasks. It was customary in the first-century Middle East for the elder son to stand at the door barefoot to greet the guests, which was a symbolic gesture by which the father is saying to the villagers, "My older son is your servant" (Bailey, p. 194).

The elder son did not go about his protest regarding his younger brother in the proper manner. Culturally, it would have been proper for the son, if he had a disagreement with his father, to first enter the house and fulfill his role as the host. He was expected publicly to embrace and welcome his brother back and to receive the compliments that will be paid to him by his guests who assume that he is glad to have his brother back. He was expected to show recognition to his brother as the honored guest. When the party was over and all had left, then it would have been the proper time for the elder son to share his grievance with his father. Instead, the son decided to quarrel with his father while the guests were present and thereby humiliated the father publicly. Bailey points out that customs in the Middle East with its high regard for the father make the older son's action all that more insulting and out of place. But it is an insult in any culture for a family to host a banquet and at the same time for the elder son to have a public quarrel with his father.

There is now a break in the relationship between the father and the elder son. The elder son's path to the banquet hall is step by step a parallel to the road just traveled by the younger son. The father seems to be going from crisis to crisis. For the second time in the same day the father goes down and out of his house, presenting in public humiliation unexpected love. The father is no less anxious for the elder son to return, not to scold or rebuke, as one may expect, but to entreat him just as he had his younger son. One would expect that such a demonstration of unexpected love for the older son would have the same effect as it did on the younger son. Unfortunately, we never get to know the final outcome.

By now most of the guests at the party know that the family is having a serious problem. Instead of the father being with his guests and newly-found son celebrating the most joyous time in his life, he is out in the backyard having a heated discussion with his elder son. By the elder son's speech we can deduct a great deal about the son and his feelings toward his father and his brother. By saying to his father, "I have slaved for you," he is revealing that he has been living in the house with an attitude of a slave, not with the familiarity of a son. His whole perception has been warped by his attitude. He has just publicly humiliated his father and yet he is able to say to his father with a straight face, "I have never disobeyed you." Notice that the elder son addresses his father without title. Up to this point titles are used in the parable in direct speech. The sudden absence of any title is an obvious lack of respect on the elder son's part.

At this point the difference between the two sons was that the younger son was estranged and rebellious while leaving home, and the older son was estranged and rebellious in his heart while he remained at home. The rebellion in the heart of the younger was evident in his desire to leave his father and brother. The elder son's estrangement and rebellion were evident in his anger and his refusal to enter into the celebration. Both rebel. Both break the father's heart. Both end up in a far country — one physically and one spiritually. And the father, embarrassed by the actions of both sons, in acts of humiliation and love comes out to both of them.

The older son accuses his father of favoritism by saying, "He gets a fatted calf and I don't even get a goat." He is convinced that by these actions the father has revealed how much more he cares for his younger son. The younger son revealed his feelings to his father and left. The older son remained in the house all the time hating his father. When he says, "This son of yours," instead of, "My brother," he is in essence removing himself from the family. The distance between himself and his family is further seen when the brother declares that his friends do not include his brother, his father, or any of the family's guests. Bailey's conclusion is correct, "His community is somewhere else" (p. 199).

For the second time the father is challenged as to how he is going to respond to one of his children. This time the father's integrity has been attacked. Bailey has pointed out that the father could have ordered the older son to enter the house. And he would have obeyed. But what would he gain? He did not want another servant; he wanted a son. It has been pointed out that the father bypasses the bitterness, the arrogance, the insult, the distortion of facts, and the unjust accusations. There is no judgment, no criticism, no rejection, but only an outpouring of love.

Notice, in contrast to his younger son, the father begins his speech with a title: "Son, you are always with me, and all that is mine is yours. But we had to celebrate and rejoice, because this brother of yours was dead and has come from life, he was lost and has been found" (vv. 31-32). The father addresses him as "Son." Scholars have noted by using the word *teknon* — meaning literally child — that he is using a term of love and endearment. Just as the father was compassionate toward the younger son, so is he here toward the elder. In this speech the father is telling his son what the content of his joy should be in contrast to what it is. The return of his younger brother in no way would affect his rights in any manner whatsoever. He made a clear statement to his son: "You are my heir. You own everything already. All that is mine is yours. How can I possibly give you more?" This is a remarkable scene indeed. The elder son fails to recognize that the father is always on his side and that he has no need to earn his father's approval. He already has it. Scott states that "he has made himself a slave for something that was already his" (*Hear Then The Parables*, p. 121).

Note, the audience views the elder son as selfish and self-righteous, but the father addresses him with compassion by saying, "Son." This is the difference between how the world sees a person and how God views him/her. The world's response is one of contempt and disregard, but God's response is one of love and acceptance. Shillington points out that in the Middle East old men do not entreat their sons. They order them. To beg is demeaning and indicates a lack of shame. The father's behavior to both of his sons was a shock to the village (*Jesus And His Parables*, p. 160). But he is not your ordinary father, because the father's number one priority in this whole affair is family reconciliation. Notice that the father's speech is neither an apology for the banquet nor a reproach directed against the older brother, but primarily a cry from the heart for an understanding of grace. Gently, but forcefully the father reminds his son, "This is your brother who was dead and has come to life; he was lost and has been found." In regard to both sons, the father did not do what many would have considered the just thing — punish the sons for their rebellious acts and attitudes. Rather he offers each of them love and grace. The result of the father's love is that the younger son who was dead is now alive. The older son is likewise dead, but the question is will he come to life?

The elder son's weakness is that he saw his relationship with his father as one of duty. Therefore, his life became burdensome, dull, and without joy. The sins of the saints are usually the sins of disposition, but nonetheless destructive, especially in regard to relationships. Such stay-at-home prodigals become critical when they should be supportive, censorious when they should be compassionate. They become arguably the church's greatest liability. It is this attitude that undermines the life and vitality of many churches. I can sympathize with the pastor who feels that his church is just one or two funerals from breaking loose into new life. Moses had the same problem. He had to wander in the wilderness until some of the "nay-sayers" died off and then he made his way to the promised land. A critical negative attitude can kill a church and rob it of its spirit.

The story ends abruptly. It does so with good reason. Jeremias has pointed out that the issue is still open. In this way we may recognize the reality of the situation which confronted Jesus. Those who were listening to the parable were in the position of the elder brother who had to decide whether he would accept his father's invitation and share in his joy. The Pharisees who had raised the question about Jesus eating with sinners, which was the reason for Jesus telling this narrative in the first place, were left to ponder their question in light of the story that they had just heard. Jesus ends his story with hope. He hopes that those who hear it, those who were so critical of his table companions, of his befriending sinners and outcasts, would turn from their critical and loveless attitude and come to experience the great joy that the gospel seeks to bring to them.

The curtain drops on the drama and the son is still outside. Did the father succeed in convincing him or did he remain outside?

Also the Pharisees now had to give their answer to the question as well. Therefore the end of parable is determined by the listener's/reader's response. We have all wandered from our heavenly father's house. We are all prodigals. We have spurned God's law, we have ignored God's love, and we have polluted God's creation. Everyone must decide how he or she will respond to God's love. Our response will determine the nature of the parable's conclusion.

Discussion Questions

1. **Identity.** Why did Jesus include the story of the elder son in the parable? Do you agree that Jesus included the section on the elder son because most of us identify with it? Isn't it true that most prodigals stay home and pout rather than running off in a huff to a distant land? Where do you see yourself in this parable?

2. **Attitude.** Do you agree that the older brother's sins of disposition and attitude were less obvious but potentially more destructive to the family? If you were to describe the elder son today what characteristics would he have? Would he be highly respected in your community?

3. **Stranger.** The question has been asked, how could this elder son remain at home, live in his father's house and become the recipient of his father's love, yet drift so far, from his father that he became a stranger in his own house? Is it possible for people to be lifetime members of the church and not have the slightest idea of what is going on? Do they undermine the cause of the gospel, as well as, the task of the church?

4. **Resentment.** The elder son seemed to be jealous of his younger brother, resenting the treatment he was receiving from his father. Do you find yourself resenting the good fortune which comes to another by sheer grace?

5. **Criticism.** Jesus told this parable to those who criticized him for eating and associating with sinners and publicans. Does the church risk any criticism by embracing the disreputable in God's name today? Why did Jesus end this parable as he did?

Prayer

I confess, O God,
that often I let my mind wander down unclean and forbidden ways;
that often I deceive myself as to where my plain duty lies;
that often, by concealing my motives, I pretend to be better than I am;
that often my honesty is only a matter of policy;
that often my affection for my friends is only a refined form of caring for myself;
that often my sparing of my enemy is only a refined form of caring for myself;
that often I do good deeds only to be seen by others, and shun evil ones only because I fear they may be found out.
O holy One, let the fire of thy love enter my heart, and
burn up this coil of meanness and hypocrisy, and
make my heart as a heart of a child. Amen.

— From *A Diary of Private Prayer*, John Baillie

Chapter 8

A Story That Never Ends

This story of two lost sons and a loving father is one of rebellion, disrespect, selfishness, and greed. Above all, it is the powerful story of love and grace. It is the story of a lost son: lost to his father, lost to his family, lost to his community, and lost to his heritage. It tells of an older son who remained at home and became a stranger in his own house. Because of the relentlessness of a father's love and the fact that a lost son could not obliterate or deny his roots or forget what life was like in the father's house, it ends in a joyful homecoming. As long as there are parents and children, there will always be rebellion, anger, pain, and the running away into a distant land. Because of the persistence of love and grace that can reach to the farthest land and forgive the gravest sin — there will always be a homecoming. It is a story that never ends, because there is no end to the love and grace of God that seeks to bring the wanderer home.

This great parable has many themes working its way through the story. First, it is a story of joy. It is a story of great joy because it is a love story. It speaks about a love that existed before any rejection was possible and a love that will still be there when all rejections have taken place. Nouwen reminds us that it is first the everlasting love of God who is father and mother. "Jesus' whole life and preaching had only one aim: to reveal this inexhaustible, unlimited motherly and fatherly love of God and to show the way to let that love guide every part of our daily lives" (*The Return of the Prodigal*, p. 102). Love is the source of the story's joy. The joy results because the lost son who was dead is alive again; he was lost and is found. There is the joy of the father who is reunited with his lost son. The story is a vivid picture of Jesus' joyful life-giving ministry to the lost. This is the heart of the gospel message that Jesus wants to get across to the Pharisees and scribes listening to this story. By bringing the lost, dead, and dreary souls to the joy of God's grace and love, Jesus is expressing the very nature and purpose of his ministry. The Pharisees listened to the story with a critical ear. They were greatly annoyed that Jesus would express such joy in being with sinners and publicans who became his friends. They were extremely critical of his hospitality regarding such people and they caustically stated, "This fellow welcomes sinners and eats with them." Joy was not part of their religious life. They knew the law, regulations, and rules. They knew little about love, grace, and joy. They were clueless about the meaning of heaven rejoicing over a sinner who repents or the joy of a lost son being found.

The Pharisees and scribes standing in the crowd that day had lost the wonder of life and knew nothing about joy. They were given to criticism, becoming narrow and bitingly sarcastic and calling Jesus a winebibber and glutton because he ate with sinners and took his food with gladness. The listeners are like the old professor in Ingmar Bergman's film *Wild Strawberries,* who dreamed one night he was taking an early morning walk in the empty streets of his town when a funeral procession turned into the churchyard just ahead of him. Just as the wagon bearing the coffin made the sharp turn to enter the church yard, a wheel wrenched loose and the coffin rolled off at his feet, dislodging the corpse. Left alone in the street with the body, the professor reluctantly took hold of it to put it back in the box. But a strange thing happened: the corpse seized his arm and struggled with him until they stood face to face. In horror, the professor looked into the face of the dead man. It was his own. When he woke from the dream, the professor knew the meaning of it at once. He had been living as a dead man. He was a living, walking corpse. Wonder and joy were absent from his life. He was determined to change things.

Little did these listeners realize how dead their lives had become by their attitudes of criticism and faultfinding and losing their sense of wonder and joy. Jesus had them in mind all the time he was telling this story. Would grace and love break through the crust of their hard-hearted countenance? Religion for them had become a drab and boring imposition. In John Steinbeck's *East of Eden,* his character Liza exemplifies such behavior. She is described as "a tiny Irish wife, a tight hard little woman, humorless as a chicken. She had a dour Presbyterian mind and a code of morals that pinned down and beat the brains out of nearly everything that was pleasant to do." Did Jesus ever get through to them? The story ends with that question unanswered.

Let us not overlook the fact that this story is a source of joy for God. Nouwen reminds us that God rejoices, not because the problems of the world have been solved, not because all human pain and suffering has come to an end, nor because great multitudes have been converted. No, God rejoices because one of his children who was lost is found. We are invited by God to enter into this joy. This was something the Pharisees and the scribes, who were listening to the parable, were unable to do. It is God's joy, not the kind of joy the world offers. It is the joy that comes from seeing a child walk home amid all the destruction, devastation, and anguish of the world. "From God's perspective, one hidden act of repentance, one little act of selfless love, one act of true forgiveness is all that is needed to bring God from his throne to run to the returning son and to fill the heavens with the sound of joy" (p. 108).

Jesus describes how the return of one sinner causes rejoicing in heaven and in the heart of God. This is a small joy when we consider all of those who are still outside of the father's house. Yet it is these small joys that reveal to us the truth about the world we live in. When Jesus speaks of joy, he also is realistic about his world. He talked about wars, revolutions, earthquakes, famine, persecution, imprisonment, betrayal, and death. Regardless, the joy of God can be ours in the midst of it all. Jesus' joy came from living in the father's house. This joy is not a joy without sorrow, but a joy in the midst of sorrow. Jesus was a man of sorrow acquainted with grief, but also a man of complete joy. Jesus knew about the world's sorrow, but in the midst of such a world of contradictions he shares the good news of hope, "so that my own joy may be in you and your joy be complete." The return of a child to the father's house is God's joy and our joy as well. Henri Nouwen says:

111

There is seldom a minute in my life that I am not tempted by sadness, melancholy, cynicism, dark moods, somber thoughts, morbid speculations, and waves of depression. And often I allow them to cover up the joy of my father's house. But when I truly believe that I have already returned and that my father has already dressed me in a cloak, ring, and sandals, I can remove the mask of my sadness from my heart and dispel the lie it tells about my true self and claim the truth with the inner freedom of the child of God.   — p. 110

Second, this is a parable of hope. The parable gives a clear description of what it means to be lost, yet hope shines through. Although Jesus describes in vivid terms the younger son as being lost in a distant land, at the same time, he is describing lost humanity in general. We all identify with this lostness. We have all acted in an outrageous, selfish, and rebellious manner against a loving God. We have ignored God's laws, rejected God's love, and misused God's gracious and good creation. The result is that we have been exiled to a distant land, far away from the father's house. There is good reason to view the son's rebellion as Jesus' diagnosis of the human condition in general. The parable describes our human journey in vivid terms: rebellion, greed, selfishness, disrespect, judgment, yet with the hope of self-discovery and the possibility of a joyful homecoming. The homecoming is the intent of the gospel. The gospel's intent is not to condemn but to restore, not to exile, but to bring home, forever holding on to the possibility of transformation. The hallmark of the gospel is the changed life. It is not the rebellious son living in a pig sty in a distant land, but the son coming home, being embraced by his father who throws a party to celebrate his son's return. Regardless how far we have wandered from the father's house, because of the grace of God that knows no bounds, there is the hope of a homecoming.

Third, above all it is a parable of grace. There is one theme that overrides all others in this story — it is the theme of grace. It is described by the actions of the father in regard to his rebellious sons. It is the undeserved, unmerited, unearned love of the father toward his wayward sons. On two occasions the father came out from his house in humiliation to extend his gracious love to his sons who treated him with insult and disrespect. Though treated with disgrace, the father was gracious with his love and forgiveness. The word *grace* never appears in this story, but there has never been a clearer or more forceful description of grace. Within the biblical texts, grace is expressed through stories and relationships rather than vocabulary. Neither did Jesus ever use the word *grace,* but his life was the source of its meaning. Grace happens!

Behind all of our divisions, beyond all of our famous gaps — generation, sex, credibility, ideology, political — there is a common human search for the renewing and sustaining power that only grace can provide. The Apostle Paul expressed this grace remarkably when he declared, "In Christ, God was reconciling the world to himself." In God's love, manifested in Christ, a new spiritual power has been set loose in the lives of men and women. In Christ the deepest of human needs was met: the need to be loved and accepted. The parable has expressed this in very dramatic and unforgettable terms. Fred Craddock reminds us that the story has a power all of its own. Let it stand alone and do its work on and in the hearts of the hearers.

The reason the parable has such universal appeal is because the single most compelling need of our lives is acceptance. Many times we are tormented by the notion that we need to be acceptable before we can be accepted. The prodigal sought to make himself acceptable by crafting a speech that he would present to his father on his arrival home. Grace is the beginning of our healing because it offers us the one thing we need most, acceptance, without regard to whether we are acceptable or not. For many this becomes a stumbling block regarding the gospel, because it just sounds too good to be true. However, grace means that we are *accepted* before we become *acceptable.* The Apostle Paul expressed this as, "While we were yet sinners Christ died for us." That was the prodigal's greatest discovery. Before he could ever get his speech out, before he could make himself acceptable, his father ran to him, kissed him, hugged him, and in a moment of joyful, tearful reunion, accepted his son home. It was not a question of being smart enough, clean enough, handsome enough, or good enough, or whether he had accomplished enough. The fact that he came home seeking acceptance was all that mattered. The fact is, cleaning ourselves up is the very thing we cannot do. In our helpless state, the miracle of grace brings acceptance. This is indeed amazing grace!

The story has been told that on Palm Sunday morning, April 9, 1865, General Robert E. Lee put on his finest dress uniform, mounted Traveller, and rode away from his tired and tattered troops to Appomatox, where he would surrender his beaten army to General Ulysses Grant. As Lee rode to meet his conqueror, he fully expected that his men would be herded like cattle into railroad box cars and then sent to a Union prison and he, as their general, would be tried and executed as a disgraced traitor. In the tidy living room of the home where the vanquished and the victor met, Lee asked Grant what his terms of surrendered were to be. Grant told Lee that his men were free to take their horses with them and go back to their little farms and that Lee too was free to go home and create a new life. Lee offered Grant his sword. Grant refused it. Lee heaved a sigh. He came expecting to he humiliated, and he left with dignity and honor. As he watched General Lee mount Traveller and ride back to his troops, Grant took off his hat and saluted his defeated enemy. It was a magnificent act of grace. It deeply affected the defeated general as long as he lived. Lee never allowed a critical word of Grant to be spoken in his presence. The point is this, in grace God does not give us what we deserve, rather God gives us what we need — acceptance. It is the incredible voice of our heavenly father's heart that overtakes us in a far country and tells the incredibly joyful good news, "You can come home. Come home!" Thielicke reminds us that the ultimate theme of the story is not the lost son, but the father who finds him. The ultimate theme is not the faithlessness of men and women but the faithfulness of God.

In telling the story of the prodigal's return, Jesus has drawn the most winsome picture of the grace of God. It is a vivid picture of a God who is eager to forgive utterly and to restore completely. Jesus wants to make it clear that the God of whom he speaks is a God of compassion who joyously welcomes all repentant sinners into his house. Jesus believed that by eating and socializing with people, considered by many of the religious elite as unclean and unworthy of association, he was living out God's teaching in everyday life. Nouwen states that one of the important points that Jesus is making in this parable is: If God is forgiving sinners and welcoming them home, then those who claim to be God's followers should do the same. If God loves sinners, then certainly those who love God should love in the same manner. Jesus announces the grace, love, and compassion of God, who has offered himself as an example and model for all human behavior.

The parable abruptly ends, leaving us to wonder: Did the Pharisees, the listeners, get the point of the parable? But the greater question is: Do we?

Discussion Questions

1. **Purpose.** Jesus' life, his teaching, and his preaching had one aim and purpose: to reveal the inexhaustible, unlimited love of God and to reveal how this love could guide and influence every aspect of our daily lives. How did Jesus accomplish that purpose in this parable? Did he accomplish that purpose in your live?

2. **Joy.** The parable is one of joy. The Pharisees and the scribes, who were listening with a critical ear to what Jesus had to say, did not seem to possess much joy. They were annoyed by the company that Jesus kept and that he did so with joy. They were the religious leaders, but joy was not part of their lives. How do you deal with such joyless, clueless, critical souls in our churches today?

3. **Hope.** The parable is one of hope. It expresses the hope that there will always be a homecoming. Our hope does not mean the absence of turmoil or conflict but hope in the midst of turmoil. How can Christian hope prevail for the majority of the world's population that suffer from war, life in refugee

camps, AIDs, and a grinding and debilitating poverty? Where is hope when there is so much corporate crime and ruthless political power? What do you say to the hopeless around you?

4. **Grace.** Grace is the central theme of this parable. However, the word *grace* is never mentioned. How then is grace expressed in the parable? How would you define the word *grace*?

5. **Gracious.** If God forgives sinners, then those who have faith in God should do the same. If God is compassionate, then those who love God should be compassionate. If God desires a homecoming for everyone, regardless of who or what they are, so should we. But do we? God has extended his grace, which is unmerited, undeserved, and unearned, to you through Jesus Christ. Are you so gracious and loving to others?

Prayer

O Lord, I stand amazed by your gift of grace. A sinner such as I, who has no claim upon you, yet you have extended your grace to me freely, a grace unearned, unmerited, undeserved, but freely given regardless of how far I have traveled from the Father's house. Such grace is amazing.

"And can it be that I should gain an interest
in the Savior's blood?
Died he for me? Who caused his pain!
For me? Who him to death pursued?

"Amazing love! How can it be that thou
my God, shouldst die for me?

"Amazing love! How can it be that thou
my God, shouldst die for me?" Amen.
— From Charles Wesley in *The United Methodist Hymnal*

Appendix

The Task Of Interpretation

The dominant questions for twenty centuries have been, "Do the parables express more than one point?" Do we allegorize or not? For the first nineteen centuries the Christian church used allegory as the means of interpreting the parables. Allegory in one form or another was the chief key to interpretation. Jeremias pointed out that early after the death of Jesus the parables had undergone a certain amount of interpretation. At a very early stage the parables were given to allegorical interpretation. The words of Jesus in Mark 4:10-12 have caused a great deal of controversy through the years. It has been one of the most difficult passages in the New Testament to interpret. This passage suggests that the parables concealed a mystery about the Kingdom of God from outsiders, which led to a predominance of the allegorical method of interpretation. Throughout this period the allegory grew as the means of interpretation. Tertullian (160-220) encouraged the use of allegory as seen in his famous sermon on the Prodigal Son, which reveals allegory at its best and worse. Origen (185-254) was called the "maestro" of allegorical interpretation. Augustine (354-430) was masterful in his use of allegorical interpretation, especially in his sermon on the Good Samaritan, which became the standard for centuries. For nineteen centuries church leaders felt that Jesus was using parables as a *coded message,* clear to some and obscure to others. From the Apostolic Age, to the Middle Ages, through the Reformation, and up to the end of the nineteenth century, the allegorical interpertation of the parables prevailed in the Christian church.

Allegorical Interpretation Challenged

It was not until the end of the nineteenth century that a radical break was made in this approach to interpretation. Adolf Julicher in his work, *The Parables of Jesus,* in 1888, sounded the death knell to the allegorical interpretation of the parables. He felt the parables of Jesus were pedagogical tools to impart general moral and religious principles. Julicher was convinced that a parable had only one central point and the remaining details were supporting material. The weakness of his approach was his insistence that the parables had only one point and this one point should be given as general and broad interpretation as possible. His critics felt this greatly dulled and flattened the meaning of the parables.

C. H. Dodd made exegetical history with his book *The Parables of the Kingdom* in 1935. He pointed out that the Gospels themselves gave encouragement to the allegorical method of interpretation. Mark in his Gospel interprets the Parable of the Sower and Matthew in his Gospel those of the Tares and the Dragnet allegorically. Both authors attribute their interpretation to Jesus. For Dodd the realism of the parables is remarkable in their understanding between nature and human life, between natural order and the spiritual order. For him, Jesus can take any part of the natural order and find that it illumines the other parts of creation and human life. This sense of divineness of the natural order is the major premise of all the parables, and for Dodd it is the point where Jesus differs most profoundly from the outlook of the Jewish apocalyptists. Dodd put the parables back into their true setting — where the ministry of Jesus is seen as the great echatological act of God in which God visited and redeemed his people.

Dodd was interested in examining the parables on two levels: that of the ministry of Jesus and that of the early church. He argued that to retain the true vitality of the parable it was essential to interpret it in the context of the historical crisis that Jesus' presence and activity brought about. For Dodd, the central meaning of Jesus' parables was the meaning of the kingdom of God as the central point in the Gospel and the parables; the reign of God in the coming kingdom was the great hope of the future; and in Christ the kingdom of God had arrived and invaded history in Jesus' person and mission.

Joachim Jeremias has had a profound influence on the study of the parables in this century with his book, *The Parables of Jesus* (1947). He rejected Julicher's universalizing interpretations of the parables in favor of one that anchored them in specific, historical

118

situations. He felt that allegory is an inferior form of rhetoric, unworthy of Jesus, who instead was master of the metaphor. He felt that the parables have a twofold historic setting: one, the original historic setting; second, the historic setting of the primitive church. He was convinced that the second setting is the only one we can know. The primitive church related the parables to its own actual situation, which he felt was characterized by the Gentile environment, the Gentile mission, and the delay of the *Parousia*. He felt that the primitive church setting often produced a change in meaning, in particular, by the addition of generalizing conclusions, which caused the parables to acquire a universal meaning. Dodd and Jeremias sought to put the parables of Jesus back into their true setting, which is the ministry of Jesus as seen as the great act of God being in Christ seeking to bring the world to himself. Both felt that the heart of the parables' message was that God's royal intervention into the world was not some shining hope on the distant horizon, but that the time had fully come; in Jesus the kingdom had arrived, and in Jesus, God was invading history. They saw the coming of the kingdom in the ministry of Jesus as *realized eschatology*. Up until the middle of the twentieth century Dodd and Jeremias were the outstanding authorities regarding the study of the parables. However, Dodd's and Jeremias' postions have been seriously challenged by the research of Craig L. Blomberg in his book, *Interpreting the Parables* (InterVarsity Press, 1990).

Views Regarding Interpretation

The significance of biblical scholarship in the twentieth century regarding the study of the parables has been to differentiate sharply between parables and allegories. Most survey courses today on the parables would probably contain most of the following assertions regarding the parables.

1. *Throughout the history of the church most Christians interpreted the parables as allegories.* The interpreters assumed that many of the individual characters and objects in the parables stood for something other than themselves — spiritual counterparts that allowed them to be read and

interpreted on two levels. The parable was not just a story about human activity but also an earthly story with a heavenly meaning. The parable does not have one central meaning, but every detail of the parable has some parallel meaning. Scholars have felt that the parable of the sower, with its descriptions not only of the seed sown, but of the different kinds of soil in which it is planted, lends itself more to allegory than parable. Also, Jesus's own interpretation of this parable gave support to allegory. Even today, there is the temptation to treat the parables as allegory.

2. *Modern scholarship has rejected allegorical interpretation in favor of an approach that recognizes that each parable makes only one point.* Scholars came to realize that through allegorical interpretation with its emphasis on every detail and giving those details parallel meaning that it severely diminished the central meaning of the parable. The allegorical method ignored the realism, clarity, and simplicity of the parables. In studying the use of allegory over the years, it became evident that it was a means of interpretation of one's favorite theme. This was evident in Martin Luther with his theological emphasis of justification by faith which kept influencing his allegorical interpretation. Luther, like those before and after him, was tempted to use allegory for his own purposes.

3. *A few of the parables in the Gospels do have allegorical elements.* Scholars believe that those parables that have allegorical tendencies (Parables of the Sower, the Tares and the Dragnet) were never spoken by Jesus, at least in the form that they now appear. Other scholars are more willing to admit the dichotomy is not so great, and that Jesus may have, on occasion, employed allegory. They suggest that the traces of allegory which do occur in the Gospel parables can be attributed to the early church's imposition of the motif of the *Messianic secret* on to the Jesus tradition. However, the allegorical parable still remains

the exception, not the norm, although recent studies by Craig Blomberg seek to reestablish the idea that most of the parables are allegories.

4. *The interpretations of the parables within the Gospels were supplied by the early church and possibly by the Gospel writers themselves.* This seems to be particularly true in regard to the Parable of the Sower. Scholars feel that since Jesus left most of his parables without such interpretation proves that they are to be taken less elaborately. Thus, the task of biblical scholarship today is to try to discover the original meaning of the parables. Scholars of the new hermeneutic, such as Drury, feel that the original meaning of any parable is beyond recall.

5. *The parables are among the most indisputably authentic sayings of Jesus.* Fully one third of all of the sayings of Jesus in the Synoptic Gospels occur in parables. Knowing the parables is essential for understanding the person of Christ. In the parables of the New Testament, we are dealing with a particularly trustworthy tradition and we are brought immediately into a relationship with Jesus. The parables represent Jesus' basic message and present us with the permanent challenge and hope of the Christian understanding of existence.

The New Hermeneutic

In recent studies in the area of the new hermeneutic, many questions have been raised in regard to the popular methods of interpretation. This school of thought alleges that the parables are neither simple stories drawn from everyday life with one particular religious truth nor allegories in which each detail represents some deep spiritual truth. Rather they are metaphors that cannot be paraphrased in prepositional language or reduced to a certain number of points.

One of the most influential scholars in this field is Bernard B. Scott and his book, *Hear Then The Parable* (1989). His study represents the approach of the Society of Biblical Literature's parable study group that began their work in the mid-1970s. Scott not only believes that it is impossible to state the original meaning of the parable, but also the parables do not point to an apocalyptic kingdom of God. He feels that the quest for the most original meaning of any given parable is misguided from the beginning, because the oral storytellers varied their stories with every performance. It is clear that there is much work to be done in trying to sift the wheat from the chaff among recent parable scholarship.

The Literary Cultural Approach

Kenneth E. Bailey brings a breath of fresh air to the study of the parables in his book, *Poet and Peasant: A Literary Cultural Approach to the Parables of Luke* (1976). He believes that the Parables present us with a *cultural problem.* When studying the parables, their theology is expressed in stories about particular people who lived in a given cultural setting at a specific time in history. To understand the theology of the parables, he feels it is necessary to re-capture the culture of first-century Palestine that informs the text. When the cultural base ceases to be first-century Palestine, the parables inevitably become stories of foreigners. This *foreignness* of the cultural that informs the parable he calls the *cultural problem.* He seeks to overcome this cultural problem by his methodology that involves 1) discussing the cultural aspects of the parables with Middle Easterners; 2) examining pertinent ancient literature; and, 3) consulting the Oriental versions of the Gospels. He could do this because he has spent most of his academic life in the Middle East as Chairman of the Biblical Department at the Near Eastern School of Theology in Beirut.

He points out that historically there have been five different approaches regarding the cultural problem. First, the church *allegorized.* This is best illustrated by Origen who allegorizes and denied culture played a part. Second, others *indigenized.* The exegete felt that first-century people were just like him, causing him to conclude "it is only reasonable to assert" or "it is only natural to assume." To which one must ask, "Reasonable to whom? Americans, Africans, Asians?" Bailey concludes, once one asks that question the fallacy of indigenization is readily recognizable. The third method is to *universalize*. The exegete assumes that all people are basically alike in human relationships. There are human problems that all people share and that all people seek to solve. But the cultural patterns for describing them and expressing them are quite different. Bailey suggests that saying that all people think alike really means that all people think like me. The fourth method is to *existentialize*. In reality, Bailey feels, this shifts the discussion from exegesis to hermeneutics. The historical question must be answered before the hermeneutical concern is addressed. One cannot discuss the language event until it is clear what language event is proposed. Without the historical question, the language event becomes the creation of the exegete. His fifth point is to *despair*. Some feel that the time gap is just too great. We are just too far removed from the Palestinian world of Jesus. The information is too scanty and the path back is too narrow. Those holding this view argue that the original meaning of the parables in their Palestinian setting is irrecoverably lost.

Bailey's response to all of this is that these alternatives are neither appropriate nor necessary. He concludes that the text of the parables can be recovered in a rather systematic fashion. This means of recovery is what he calls *Oriental exegesis*. His approach to this field of study requires an examination of the culture of contemporary conservative peasants to see what the parables mean in their setting. Oriental texts need to be studied to see how the Oriental church people through the centuries have translated the text. Ancient literature pertinent to the parables must be read with the insights gained from these other two sources, not isolated from them. He states that the text must be examined against the background information gleaned from these relevant sources.

How Do We Interpret The Parable Of The Prodigal Son?

Where do we go from here? Interpreters of the parables today face a bewildering array of methods from which to choose. Scholarship is becoming much more fragmented and specialized, leaving the non-specialists baffled as to where to turn and what to choose. Nevertheless, every method has made an important contribution. My approach to the study of the Parable of the Prodigal Son is that the parable contains one central theme and I do not treat the parable as an allegory. I feel there is a case for the reconstruction of the parables, although the new hermeneutic school states that the reconstruction of the parables may be impossible to achieve. I will give close attention to those who seek to reconstruct the parable as to the setting and the meaning that the parable had for the first hearers, because this is essential in order to gain the contemporary meaning of the parable.

My criticism of the new hermeneutic is that they have abandoned the search for what the parables meant to the first-century hearers and are willing to accept them as disembodied "works of art" with a new set of general meanings, causing them to lose their force and power. This is exactly the same mistake that Julicher had made a century earlier. Bailey and his "literary-cultural" approach to the parables in the Gospel of Luke have been extremely helpful to me in gaining first-century insight to the meaning of the Parable of the Prodigal Son. Bailey has been the antithesis to the new hermeneutic school showing that reconstruction is possible. The case for reconstruction has been further strengthened by Andrew Parker in his book, *Painfully Clear.*

Although in this manuscript I spend time on the textual and cultural details of the parable, I want the reader to know that I am convinced that there is one central meaning to the Parable of the Prodigal Son. The themes of this parable are sin, rebellion, remorse, repentance, grace, joy, and sonship. None of these can be dealt with in isolation. Each is seen in dynamic tension with the others. Each theme can be reflected upon separately, but to deal with one is to deal with all. The various themes of the parable give support to the parable's one major theme, which is to answer the Pharisees' question why Jesus associates with sinners.

Sources

There are several sources that I found extremely helpful and have cited them more frequently than others. This is especially true of Kenneth Bailey's *Poet and Peasant*. Because of his many years of studying and teaching in the Middle East, he brings a rich cultural and historical understanding of the text along with a keen analysis of the parables' literary style. Henri Nouwen in his *The Return of the Prodigal Son* has made a unique contribution to the study of the parable by the inspiration he received through Rembrandt's painting and how it reflects on his own life's journey. Bernard B. Scott's *Hear Then the Parable*, by his probing literary and social analysis along with his cultural insight of the text, presents us with a rich comprehensive study of the parables. Brad Young, in his book, *The Parables of Jesus: Jewish Tradition and Christian Interpretation*, presents a fresh study of the text because of his proficiency in the Hebrew and Aramaic sources of early Judaism. Robert Farrar Capon, in his *Parables of Grace*, is able to bridge the gap between the centuries and capture the meaning of the parables for modern times in an insightful, humorous, and provocative manner. Craig L. Blomberg, in his book *Interpreting the Parables*, evaluates the contemporary critical approach to the parables, challenging the prevailing consensus of C. H. Dodd and Joachim Jeremias that the parables make one central point, and he feels many are allegories. This book makes important new contributions to the study of the parables as Blomberg provides us with new insight from his distinctive method.

The following sources have been cited in this volume:
Atkins, Marguerite Henry, *Also My Journey*, as quoted by Norman Shawchuch in *A Guide to Prayer for Ministers and Other Servants*, Upper Room, 1983
Bailey, Kenneth E., *Poet and Peasant*, Eerdmans, 1976
_____, *Through the Eyes of Peasants*, Eerdmans, 1980
Barclay, William, *The Gospel of Luke*, Westminster Press, 1956
_____, *The Gospel of Mark*, Westminster Press, 1975

Blomberg, Craig L., *Interpreting the Parables*, InterVarsity Press, 1990

Brueggemann, Walter, *Hope and History*, John Knox Press, 1987

Buttrick, David, *The Mystery and Passion*, Fortress, 1992

Buttrick, George, *The Parables of Jesus*, Baker, 1990

Capon, Robert Farrar, *The Parables of Grace*, Eerdmans, 1988

Craddock, Fred, *Interpretation: Luke*, John Knox Press, 1990

Culpepper, R. Alan, *The New Interpreter's Bible*, vol. IX, Abingdon, 1995

Dodd, C. H., *The Parables of Jesus*, Scribners, 1938

Fenhagen, James C., *Invitation to Holiness*, Harper, 1985

Fisher, Neal F., *The Parables of Jesus*, United Methodist Publishing House, 1979

Fitzmyer, Joseph A., *The Anchor Bible: Luke*, vol. 28A, Doubleday, 1983

Foster, George, *Peasant Character and Personality*, Little Brown and Co., 1967

Gilmour, Maclean S., *Interpreter's Bible: Luke*, vol. 8, Abingdon, 1952

Glass, Bill, *Crime: Our Second Vietnam*, Zondervan, 1992

Gublin, Charles H., *Structural and Theological Considerations in Luke*, CBQ, 1962

Hunter, Archibald M., *Interpreting the Parables*, Westminster, 1960

Jeremias, Joachim, *Rediscovering the Parables of Jesus*, Scribners, 1955

Kidd, Sue Monk, *God's Joyful Surprise*, HarperCollins Publishers, 1989

Nouwen, Henri J. M., *The Return of the Prodigal*, Doubleday, 1992

Oesterley, W.O.E., *The Gospel Parables in Light of Their Jewish Background*, SPCK, 1936

Parker, Andrew, *Painfully Clear: The Parables of Jesus*, Sheffield, 1996

Pfifer, Kenneth G., *Book of Uncommon Prayer*, Upper Room, 1990

Sa'id, Ibrahim, *Commentary on Luke*, Near East Council of Churches, 1970

Scott, Bernard Brandon, *Hear Then the Parables*, Fortress, 1990

Shillington, George V., editor, *Jesus and His Parables*, T&T Clark, 1997

Thielicke, Helmut, *The Waiting Father*, Harper and Row, 1959

Tillich, Paul, *The Shaking of the Foundations*, Scribners, 1948

Watson, David Lowes, *God Does Not Foreclose*, Abingdon, 1990

Weatherhead, Leslie D., *Psychology, Religion, and Healing*, Abingdon Press, 1953

Wenham, David, *The Parables of Jesus*, InterVarsity Press, 1989

Westermann, Claus, *The Parables of Jesus in Light of the Old Testament*, Fortress, 1990

Young, Brad H., *The Parables of Jesus: Jewish Tradition and Christian Interpretation*, Hendrickson, 1998